MY ANCES'
WERE
CONGREGATIONALISTS

IN
ENGLAND & WALES

WITH A LIST OF REGISTERS

compiled by

D.J.H. CLIFFORD

1992

Published by
Society of Genealogists
14 Charterhouse Buildings
Goswell Rd London EC1M 7BA

First Published 1992
(c)D J H Clifford

ISBN 0 946789 46 0

ACKNOWLEDGEMENTS

This booklet could not possibly have been completed without the unstinting help of certain people and organizations. Particularly I should single out the following :

Mr F Keay of the URC Historical Society who also allowed me access to a list of chapel closures compiled by the late George Esselton; Pastor Graham Adams and his staff at Castle Gate, Nottingham; Professor Dr R.Tudur Jones for his enthusiastic assistance over the Welsh chapels; Mrs Non Davis for guiding me through 'BLWYDDIADUR' - the Welsh Independent Handbook; Mrs Susan Lumas of the PRO; Mrs Mary Gandy of the Society of Genealogists; and my own minister, Rev Dean Tapley of Christ Church URC for the loan of various reference books.

Also the many Record Offices, Libraries and Church Secretaries up and down the land who have supplied me with the information. Sincerest thanks to all !

David Clifford,Crawley,Sussex

Royalties from the sale of this booklet will be donated to the work of the Council for World Mission

INTRODUCTION

I am sure that family historians are well aware that the Parish Registers of the Church of England are not the only available source for identifying the births, marriages and burials of their forebears. The other titles in this series have made the point quite forcibly.

However, admirable as they have been, to merely record holdings at the Public Record Office and at the Society of Genealogists, seems to tell only part of the story.

It is with this in mind that I have tried to attain two targets. Firstly, all Record Offices with non-parochial holdings have been included, together with several of our major Libraries. Secondly, an almost exhaustive list of Congregational chapels has been compiled, all of which are known to have been founded before 1850. This is to merely widen the possible fields of research in line with the ever growing series 'The National Index of Parish Parish Registers', sponsored by the Society. From this series I would particularly commend Volume II by D.F.Steel entitled 'Sources for Nonconformist Genealogy and Family History'. The cut-off date of 1850 will be explained later.

Congregationalism cannot claim a founder in the way that the Presbyterian Church look on John Knox as the inspiration of their particular brand of dissenting faith. It may never be established when Congregationalism first took root, but the slight evidence that we do have seems to indicate that it is at least as old as Knox's church, which means that both denominations could well be as old as the Church of England

The accession of Queen Elizabeth I caused a reversal to the short ascendancy of Roman Catholicism during her sister Mary's reign, but it also became apparent to all people not prepared to subscribe to the Anglican Church, that persecution was far from over, and such fellowships that had been established were forced to meet in secret, fearing further reprisals. These fellowships, who became known as Separatists, were few in numbers during the mid 1550s, but we do know how one of them operated.

This group, who met in London, was led by a Richard Fitz, who had been elected as their pastor and minister. Further, two others were appointed deacons or elders, and a regular mid-week meeting to conduct the administrative affairs was established. Also we find that the members of this fellowship had decided to bind themselves together in a Solemn Covenant.

This general picture has, with very little modification, remained part of the structure of Congregationalism to this day.

Some twenty years afterwards, a group of Cambridge men led by Robert Browne of Corpus Christi College founded a Separatist church in Norwich. Browne, who had originally broken away from the sect, became the first exponent of what eventually became

Congregationalism. During a stay in the household of Richard Greenham, vicar of Dry Drayton in Norfolk and a 'sterling example of a Puritan godly pastor', Browne became convinced that a Christian had no need of a Bishop's consent to preach the Gospel, and he started to question the doctrinal basis of the Established Church's parochial system.* At the fellowship in Norwich a Covenant was made to elect officers, institute discipline in worship and to organize regular church meetings.

Sadly, the authorities retaliated, and Robert Browne and his group, who had been dubbed 'Brownists' were forced, like others of the same ideals, into exile in the Netherlands. Thereafter the story is a sad one. Dissentions within the Brownists made Robert, its leader, quit in 1584, return to England, and sign an abject form of submission to the Archbishop of Canterbury. He eventually died in gaol in 1633, a broken man.

Robert Browne however is remembered far more from the writings that he left behind. Two tracts of his - 'A Treatise of Reformation without tarying for anie, and of the wickednesse of those Preachers which will not reform till the Magistrate commaunde or compell them' and 'A Booke which Sheweth the life and manners of all true Christians' were put into general circulation, and perhaps did more than anything before to establish the ideals for which Separatists had lived and died .

When James VI of Scotland succeeded Elizabeth in 1603, he brought the Presbyterians with him ; they had prospered since his accession to the Scottish throne, and were a fairly well organised branch of the church. The Separatists were naturally hopeful of better treatment. Certainly the climate had changed to favour them, but any strong alliance with the Scots proved impossible. Almost immediately it became clear that the King was hostile to all forms of belief likely to threaten the Presbyterians, who now began to dominate Parliament. Several Anglican vicars were deprived of their livings, and the Separatists were still forced to lie low.

Several new names amongst the Separatists now emerged, in particular a John Robinson who had become a Lecturer in Norwich. Robinson joined forces with another man, John Smyth, who had settled in Gainsborough in 1605 after dismissal from a church post in Lincoln. A third man joined them, William Brewster, a former diplomat who had left the government in disgust to take up the position of postmaster of Scrooby in Nottinghamshire.

For some years before the emergence of Robinson and Smyth, Brewster had been instrumental in organizing several Puritan fellowships. However, in 1606, a new Archbishop of York, Toby Matthew , viewed the growth of Separatism as not only a threat to the Church of England, but also to the brand of Puritanism which he himself favoured. Consequently, Robinson and his friends were also forced into exile in Holland and made their headquarters in

* Greenham features in 'The Dictionary of National Biography'

2

Amsterdam. John Smyth soon left their ranks to become a Baptist, but Robinson and Brewster remained true Separatists and having moved their cause to Leyden, prospered so well, that it can be true to say that this period for them, was a happy one. A paper by Robinson, published in 1610 entitled 'A Justification of Seperatism' indicates very clearly how the thoughts and reactions of these early Independents had modified. Robinson, despite his convictions, seems unwilling to deny the validity of his original baptism by an Anglican priest, and he accepts that the Anglican clergy have just as much right to proclaim the Gospel. Later on he goes so far as to encourage members of the movement to attend Anglican churches if they so wished. But always he insisted on his dislike in the way the Church of England carried on its affairs. All this amounted to a re-statement of the Separatist position, but it was deliberately designed to open the door to closer co-operation with the other dissenting sects.

It was this modified 'semi-Separatism' as it has been termed, that was carried by the Pilgrim Fathers' in 1620, with William Brewster as their leader on their momentous voyage to the New World. It should be mentioned that although everyone associates the Pilgrims with Plymouth in Devon, the main party had been drawn from exiles in the Netherlands.

Meanwhile, in England, the Separatists still had to struggle to survive. A church was founded in Southwark, London in 1616, and it was claimed by the Bishop of Exeter in 1631, that there were eleven known Separatist congregations in London alone. However, overall the movement was very weak. The suppressions by Archbishop Laud over the next ten years did little for their fortunes, and so it was not until 1640 after thousands more had been forced over to Holland and when mounting opposition to the monarchy and the Established Church began to grow, that the way opened up for the Separatist movement to expand.

The theological ideas of the Separatists, as interpreted by the Mayflower Pilgrims, began to spread about England, as pastors from the New World returned to their homeland in the succeeding years. More and more returned from their Dutch exile adding to the numbers, and it is at this time that the movement dropped the term 'Separatist' and re-named itself 'Independent'.

Dr Tudur Jones has pointed out that it was largely due to the influence of the New World settlers that the first Independent church in Wales was founded at Llanvaches in Monmouthshire in 1639. Happily the modern inheritors of this fellowship still worship there, though now under the mantle of the United Reformed Church.*
In a like manner,the Independents in Norfolk acknowledged the influence of their exiled brethren in the Netherlands by founding a second church in Norwich in 1643.

* 'Congregationalism in England 1662-1962' - R.Tudur Jones (1962)

The English Civil War, which broke out in 1642, also released the flood-gates for the Independents. For years they had fought hard against the Episcopacy of the Established Church ; now they found that they were part of a great movement which was daily proving itself strong enough to take on the State Church and, in all probability, would win. For the next fifteen years they were also able to enjoy the privilege of worshipping in their own way without fear of reprisal.

During the War, it seems that the majority of the Independents came from the poorer classes and from the Army. Oliver Cromwell himself was a declared Independent, and although the good folk at St Ives Meeting House may claim him as perhaps their most famous Church Member, it has been suggested that he was more likely to have affiliated himself to one of the many military chapels that had sprung up following the creation of the New Model Army.*

From the outset of the Civil War it became apparent that total victory over the King and the Church was unlikely to succeed without the military support of Scotland. Scotland was of course strongly Presbyterian, and although the Scottish influence on English Government had diluted since the days of King James, they were still treated with considerable suspicion by the English dissenters.

But Cromwell's attempt at re-creating the monarchy in 1657, resulted in an outcry from all sides to the effect that Parliament was exceeding the powers laid down by the so-called Long Parliament. The Independents were at the forefront of this opposition, backed by the army, but it also gave the Presbyterians the opportunity to re-assert the powers they had had in earlier years. They succeeded in getting certain local magistrates charged for not silencing the 'many blasphemies and damnable heresies' that had appeared on all sides. This attitude caused a rift between Independent and Presbyterian which took years to heal, and it also sharply divided the Independents themselves in their response to Richard Cromwell, Oliver's son and nominated successor.

It must be remembered that during the Puritan period of rule efforts were made to replace the Anglican clergy. By 1660 some 1900 parish priests had been removed from their livings and replaced by dissenting pastors. Of these it has been computed that 171 were Independents.

With trouble again arising from opposition to Richard Cromwell, some of these dissenting pastors began to feel wary of the future ; they left their parish church, and either moved elsewhere, gathering an Independent, Presbyterian or Baptist minded flock about them, or even re-joined the Church of England.

With the restoration of the monarchy in the person of King Charles II, the Church of England once more came to the fore. In 1662 occurred the Great Ejectment, followed by the Act of

* The Lord Protector —Robert S Paul (1955)

4

Uniformity. Almost 2,000 dissenting congregations and their ministers were forced to leave the parish churches that had been their spiritual home for several years, and re-form in cottages and barns, requiring discretion and not a little secrecy.

It will be noticed that quite a number of Independent chapels date their foundations from this time. Two further Acts were introduced to restrict their endeavours even more. The Coventicle Act of 1664, and the Five Mile Act of 1665 were passd to deliberately limit the activities of all dissenters.

It must be stressed that the many foundations in 1662 and the succeeding years did not mean that a flurry of new chapel buildings appeared ; not only would their presence be noted and steps taken to suppress them, but the comparative poverty of most of the members would have made such a financial outlay impossible. It was not for another hundred years at least that purpose built chapels came to be built. There are, however, a few Quaker Meeting Houses that are still surviving from the 17th century, for due to kinder treatment they were allowed more freedom of worship.

A respite for the Three Denominations, albeit temporary, came with the Declaration of Indulgence in 1672, which permitted their ministers to be licenced. However, by so doing, it merely meant that they were in future marked out for more persecution should any troubles arise, which could be laid at their doors.

The Catholic James became King in 1685, and almost immediately the fortunes of the Roman Catholics in England improved. James was reasonable enough to attempt to do the same for the struggling dissenters. Thousands of persecuted Huguenots from France were encouraged to live in Britain, but James received little support for this from his predominantly Catholic Cabinet.

James died in 1688, and William of Orange, a staunch Protestant with his wife Mary Stuart were invited to share the throne of England. William had grown up in the Netherlands well aware of the problems that had beset the early Separatists and Baptists, who, of course had found in his country a safe haven from persecution. The Toleration Act of 1689 was introduced, which gave official recognition to the Meeting Houses of all dissenters, and which led to the establishment of over 1,000 new Nonconformist fellowships in the succeeding twenty years.

The next important date for nonconformity is 1753. Hitherto the chapels had become used to conducting their own christenings, marriages and burials (although at this time there were very few burial grounds exclusively for their use)- first secretly, but more openly since 1689. The Hardwick Act of 1753 brought them up with a jolt. It declared that only marriages conducted in Anglican churches were to be considered legal and valid. Only Quakers and Jews were exempt from its provisions, and it appears that the restriction was constantly abused by the Roman

Catholics. It meant that for the time being, the Nonconformist dissenters, that is Baptist,Independent and Presbyterians were made to marry in their local parish church, and that is where the event will, in all likelihood, be found.

It was not until 1836 that this restriction was removed, but even then a State appointed Registrar had to be present at each and every nonconformist wedding. Finally, in 1898, Nonconformist clergy were permitted to act as their own registrar, which privilege still holds to this day.

The start and development of the so-called Industrial Revolution really marked the hey-day of nonconformity in England and Wales. The movements were still essentially attractive to the working and emerging middle classes, and with the growth of industry, and therefore some wealth, an explosion of chapel building took place.

It was early in the nineteenth century that most Independents started to call themselves Congregationalists. One of the central features of the denomination has been its emphasis on the church fellowship embodied in its congregation. As has already been stated, at its heart is the Church Meeting.

Such was the strength of the Congregational movement, even before 1800, that local chapels formed County Unions, the first being Bedforsdshire in 1797. In 1832 the County bodies were formally united as the Congregational Union of England & Wales, whilst overseas missionary work was developed by the Colonial Missionary Society and the London Missionary Society.

By 1850 there were upwards of 2,000 Congregational causes in England and Wales, of which some 500 were in Wales itself, most being Welsh speaking congregations. As the century progressed the Welsh chapels in particular proliferated which led, in 1871, to these chapels forming the Union of Welsh Independents, which Union is still very active, with a membership of over 680 congregations, despite many closures over the years.

In 1972, by an Act of Parliament, the United Reformed Church (UR) came into being, in effect a union between the Presbyterian Church of England, the Congregational Union and the Churches of Christ, a very much smaller group, but with similar ideals. However, in Congregational terms, this merger can hardly be called a total success, as three further splits were created as a consequence. Over 250 churches, who felt unable to unite formed themselves into the Congregational Federation (CF), whilst a further 44 became the Evangelical Federation of Congregational Churches (EFCC). Turning full circle as it were, at least 25 other chapels declined any association whatsoever, and are now known as Independent Congregational Churches (IC). It should also be added that the Welsh Independents (WI), although affiliated to the Congregational Union, also declined to join the URC, although links are still maintained.

ABOUT THIS BOOK

The General Register Office, originally at Somerset House, now in St Catherine's House, Aldwych, London WC2B 6JP, was established in 1837. Under the Births & Deaths Registration Act followed by the Marriage Act, both passed in 1835/6, all entries for such events had in future to be registered with a local Registry Office in England & Wales.

These entries, commencing Ist July 1837, have ever since become available for public inspection at St Catherine's House.

Soon afterwards churches and chapels throughout England & Wales were asked to deposit such baptismal, marriage and burial entries they had been keeping . Those registers that were handed over are now at the Public Record Office, Chancery Lane, London WC2A 1LR.

Twenty years later another appeal was sent out, which resulted in the surrender of more registers .

So far as the Anglican Churches are concerned, this has presented little problem from a researcher's point of view, as they carried on the practice of keeping Baptismal,Marriage and Burial records, as they had done in the past. Not so the Non-Conformist Churches. It appears that to many of them, the task of laboriously writing out the details required not only smacked of authoritarianism, but it was also a chore well worth doing without. In consequence, far too many of the Independent/ Congregational chapels expressed their independence only too clearly by discontinuing the practice altogether. It must also be remembered that until 1898, as has already been stated, no Nonconformist minister was permitted to act as his own Registrar, unlike the State Church whose clergy had that privilege.

The consequence of this attitude was that the Congregational and other Nonconformist chapel records deposited at the PRO terminate in almost every instance in 1836 or 1837.

Another aspect which can be irritating, is to realise that for the first few years of the GRO Registers, it is palpably clear that not all the populace could have switched to civil registration. There are far too few entries to indicate an overall compliance.

It is with these two circumstances in mind, that I have tried to target all known Congregational chapels founded before 1850, this being a date sufficiently advanced for the St Catherine's House records to be reasonably reliable and complete.

A hopefully exhaustive gazetteer of chapels in England & Wales has been compiled, and where known, details of surviving registers and their present whereabouts have been noted.

Over eighty of the early foundations were written to in the hope that their records may be still extant, either with the chapel or in a local Record Office. This exercise has proved less than successful. However it is very possible that there do exist more early or later registers in the multitude of libraries up and down the country, and I do appeal to any who locate such records to pass the information on to the Society for possible inclusion in an up-dated edition.

The majority of the Congregational Registers deposited at the PRO can be found under ref RG4, and this reference is shown, where appropriate. The later 1857 deposits are filed under RG8.

Most of the County Record Offices now hold micro-film copies of the PRO holdings, and some also hold originals. Similarly the main Libraries such as Manchester, Birmingham, the Guildhall, the National Library of Wales, and of course the Society of Genealogists have either filmed copies or transcripts .

Dr Williams' Library in Gordon Square, London is another valuable source of information. Dr Daniel Williams, a Presbyterian minister who later became a Unitarian, had become a great collector of material about the Three Denominations. The Dissenters' Library, as it was originally known, was opened in London in 1729, some thirteen years after his death. It contains histories of many Nonconformist churches and their ministers, and included is a large collection devoted to the Congregationalists. Also included is a list of all known Congregational clergy from 1640 until 1716.

Perhaps the most interesting item, now in the PRO under ref RG5, is a collection of baptismal registers which the three main dissenting denominations, Baptists,Congregationalists and Presbyterians attempted to form. They had realised that many of their chapels had lapsed in maintaining records, and so tried to encourage a revival by asking the clergy to submit such entries. No fee was levied for this service, and from c.1713 registers were sent to the Library for safe-keeping. In 1837 these were also transferred to Chancery Lane.

Mention should also be made of the Bunhill Fields Burial Reg -isters. These date from 1713-1854, and contain many thousand Independent and Congregational names. The Registers can be inspected at Chancery Lane under refs RG4 & RG8.

It will be noticed that against many of the chapels which are still open, I have added 'Apply Ch.Sec'. There is a very real possibility that many of the nineteenth century foundations especially, may still have records which can be useful to the researcher. The Church Secretary is most likely to know what records are still available , or can possibly throw light on their present whereabouts. The chapel should also be consulted where the deposited records terminate in 1837, in case later registers are still in existence. A stamped addressed envelope may be well worth the trouble ! Addresses may be found in the appropriate Church Handbook, details of which are given later.

Another principal source of information is the Church Minute Book, which also may include lists of Church Members.

One of the chief features of Congregationalism has been its insistence that each church or chapel should be, for the most part, self-governing. Each fellowship is lead by a Minister, supported by a committee of Deacons or Elders, all elected by the Church Members. To administer the church's affairs, regular Meetings of Members and Officials were, and still are, held and, quite properly, minutes are kept of the proceedings. A regular item is a request for baptism, or a marriage, and it is for the Church Meeting to agree to such a request. Consequently the name(s) of the parties concerned are usually recorded and even though the chapel may have discontinued the use of Registers, the information usually entered and minuted can be just as revealing.

Some of these older Minute Books can be located in the various County Repositories, whilst others are surely still gathering dust in the chapel safe. Their importance to researchers should not be underestimated.

Of the chapels that have been listed, many have perforce closed over the years. Sadly, in some cases, leaving no records behind. Maybe they have been lost ; it is known that on several occasions, a change of Minister has meant that either the departing man has destroyed the records, as anyone who moves house tends to 'have a clear out', or, in one case that has come to my notice, a Church Treasurer actually absconded with the funds, and took the registers with him , never to be seen again !

Chapel closures have been mainly brought about due to decline in attendances, although in a populated area this can often lead to merging with another fellowship . One instance comes to mind, that of Pilgrim URC at Plymouth. The present church is the result of no less than four mergers between Congregational chapels of an earlier foundation.Two World Wars, and the accompanying bombing raids led to several buildings being destroyed, including their records. The 1972 merger resulting in the formation of the United Reformed Church also reduced the number of churches ; where a Congregational Chapel stood close to a Presbyterian, it was financial common sense to close one of them down.

It is a great disappointment to discover sometimes that a record of one's ancestor cannot be found in church or chapel records. However the amount of Congregational records that have survived should not be belittled or ignored. I am also sure that more records lie waiting to be discovered.

ABBREVIATIONS USED

CF = Congregational Federation; EFCC = Evangelical Federation; UR = United Reformed; IC = Independent Cong.; WI = Welsh Independent; UB = United with Baptists; UM = United with Methodists; PCW = Presbyterian Church of Wales.

Where these abbreviations are shown indicates not only the current denominational allegiance, but also, as at November 1991, that the chapel in question is still active.

SG = Society of Genealogists ; DWL = Dr Williams' Library
Z= Birth; C = Baptism; M = Marriage; D = Death; B = Burial

Further abbreviations have been used to denote a local repository, and are shown county by county. County names are as pre-1974 ; six of these have been paired as the holdings were too small to warrant separate headings - e.g. Cambridge & Huntingdon.

USEFUL ADDRESSES :

The Congregational Federation, 4,Castle Gate, Nottingham, NG1 7AS

The Evangelical Federation of Congregational Churches,
          10,Willow Grove, Beverley, N.Humberside, HU17 8DS

The United Reformed Church, 86,Tavistock Place, London, WC1H 9RT

The Union of Welsh Independent Churches,
          Ty John Henry, 11,Hoel Sant Helen, Swansea, SA1 4AL

BIBLIOGRAPHY
    Congregationalism in England 1662-1962, Dr R Tudur Jones
    The Story of Congregationalism, E R Routley
    The Congregational Year Book 1846-1971 (CUEW)
    The Congregational Year Book 1971- (CF)
    The URC Year Book 1972-
    Blwyddiadur - the Welsh Independent Year Book
    Sources for Nonconformist Genealogy,Vol 2 of NIPR,D F Steel
    Understanding the History & Records of Nonconformity -
                    P Palgrave-Moore,BA FSA FSG

ENGLAND

BEDFORDSHIRE

```
                    B = Bedford County Record Office
RG4/
            AMPTHILL,Maulden (1768-1872)
227              C 1730-1837,B 1785-1797 ; C 1730-1837 (B/SG)
            BEDFORD,Bunyan Meeting IC(1650)
272 & 4272       Z 1785-1837,B 1785-1797;C 1785-1837,1848-61,
                 B 1785-1828,1846-55 (B)
            BEDFORD,Howard UR(1772)
271              ZC 1769-1837,B 1790-1837;  C 1821-50,M 1837,
                                           B 1790-1850(B/SG)
            CARDINGTON,UR(1839)  formerly Baptist
274              ZC 1784-1837; copies B
            COTTON END  closed 1885, no trace of Registers
            EGGINTON (1809-40) joined with Hockliffe
            ELSTOW IC(1811) . Registers with Bunyan Meeting
            GOLDINGTON IC(1825) . Registers with Bunyan Meeting
            HARROLD UR(1809)
225              C 1800-36 ; copies B
            HOCKLIFFE (1809), now closed.
226/296          ZC 1808-36 ; C 1808-36,1847-1925(B)
            KEMPSTON IC(1840)  Registers with Bunyan Meeting
            LUTON,Union Chapel(1836)  now closed,no trace of Regs
            OAKLEY (1825)  now closed, no trace of Regs
            POTTESGROVE,Union Chapel (1838)  now closed
            POTTON (viv 1850) now closed, no trace of Regs
            ROXTON CF(1808)
2145             ZC 1824-37 ; copies B/SG
            STAGSDEN (1821) Appeared closed by 1850.No trace
            SHILLINGTON CF(1840)                   Apply Ch.Sec
            TODDINGTON,Bethel (1816) Ind. later Baptist
                      Church Minutes 1816-1953 (B)
            TURVEY (1828) UR
267              C 1828-36 ; copies B
            WRESTLINGWORTH EFCC(1813)  ; no early Registers
            WOBURN (1789-1949)
278              ZCB 1791-1837 ; copies B
```

BERKSHIRE

```
                    R = County Record Office,Reading
RG4/        ABINGDON UR(1700)
2393-6           C 1780-1837,DB 1780-1836
281-2
            ASTON TIRROLD UR(1662)
2507/283         C 1738-1837,B 1763-1837 ;  C 1738-1939,B 1734-
                 1870(R),B 1734-1870(SG)

            BRACKNELL UR(1810)
                 C 1814-1932,B 1822-1859(R)
            BUCKLEBURY CF(1811)  . no Records.before 1872
            ECCHINSWELL (1812-1968) no trace of Registers.
            FARINGDON UR(1812)
284              ZC 1803-37
            GORING & SOUTHSTOKE IC(1786)  no records before 1862
```

13

```
         HUNGERFORD UR(1806)
232          ZC 1776-1837,B 1819-30 ; C 1803-37(SG)
         MAIDENHEAD UR (1662)
Various      ZC 1769-1817,C 1808-37,B 1791-1801;
             C 1769-89,1809-19,B 1791-1811,1834(R)
         NEWBURY,Lower Meeting UR (1662)
310/299      C 1695-1771,1784-1837,B 1784-1836 ; ZC 1695-1837(SG)
         PANGBOURNE UR (1824)
88           ZC 1834-36
         PEPPARD CF   (1798)  no early Registers.
         READING,Broad St (1662-1936)
2509/489     Z 1715-86,C 1765-1837,DB 1759-75,B 1787-1837;
             C 1786-1844,B 1787-1869(R) ; ZC 1695-1837(SG)
         READING,Ebenezer (1819-1930)
236          C 1820-29
         READING,London St (1820-27)
4004         ZC 1821-24
         READING,Rokeby  Hall  UR (1829)          Apply  Church
Sec.
         SLOUGH UR (1835) no Records before 1850
         SLOUGH,Chalvey UR (1806) no records before 1850
         THATCHAM UR (1804)
89           C 1807-36,B 1819-21
         THEALE UR (1832)  no early records
         TILEHURST UR (1797)  no registers before 1889
         TWYFORD UR (1794)
             C 1812-26,1836-46(R)
         WALLINGFORD (1785)  combined with Benson c1885
61           ZC 1788-1837,B 1814-36 ; ZC 1788-1812 (R)
         WANTAGE,Back Chapel (1730) closed by 1845
238          ZC 1833-34
         WINDSOR,William St (1778) now closed
290          Z 1781-1836,B 1833-37
         WOOLHAMPTON(viv 1850) now closed,no trace of records.
```

BUCKINGHAMSHIRE

```
                    A = County Record Office Aylesbury
RG4/
         AMERSHAM,Lower Meeting (1662). now closed
             C 1773-1837,B 1784-137(DWL) ; C 1776-1813 (SG)
         ASTON ABBOTTS (1839-1927)  no trace of records
         ASTWOOD (1804-1962) no trace of records
         AYLESBURY,Hale Leys UR(1707)
240          ZC 1789-1837,DB 1790-1837 ; C 1789-1850,M 1838-48,
             B 1791-5,1817-83(A) ; C 1789-1837,B 1807-37(DWL)
         AYLESBURY,Bethesda (1800) now closed,no trace
         BEACONSFIELD,Old Meeting UR(1720)
241          ZC 1785-1837 ; C 1765-1888,D 1813-25(A) ;
             C1765-1837(DWL)
         BOURNE END UR (1768)                    Apply Ch.Sec
         BOW BRICKHILL (1800-1956). no trace of records
         BRILL (viv 1850) no trace of records
         BUCKINGHAM,Old Meeting UR (1700)
293          ZC 1764-1837 ; C 1785-1837(A/DWL)
         BUCKINGHAM,Church St United with Old Meeting c1850
411          ZC 1792-1837 ; C 1792-1837 (A/DWL)
         BURCOTT (1840) Joined with Wing before 1850  no trace
         BURNHAM UR (1790)
             CMB 1843-51,CB 1858+(A)
```

```
                CHALFONT St GILES UR (1762)
                    C 1767-1811,1813-36(A/DWL): Members List 1812-50 +
                    some burials 1806+ (A)
                CHALFONT St PETER,Gold Hill Chapel. Now closed
                    C 1779-1836,B 1782-89,1821-36(DWL)
                CHESHAM High St  UR (1724)
245-8               ZCB 1786-1818,ZC 1820-37,B 1779-1836 ; copies A
                CHIPPING WYCOMBE,Ebenezer (1820) Now closed
602                 ZC 1822-36 ; copies A
                CRAWLEY,NORTH (1789-1968). No trace of records
                EDGCOTT (1825-1923) No trace of records
                GREAT HORWOOD EFCC (1821)
319                 ZC 1821-37 ; copies A
                GREAT LINFORD (1813-1967) No trace of records
                HAMBLEDON (1807) Now closed
145                 ZC 1810-36,B 1810 ; copies A
                HIGH WYCOMBE,Credden Lane (1662-1923) Now merged with
                Trinity UR
146                 ZC 1762-1836 ; copies A
                HORWOOD - see Great Horwood
                MARLOW UR (1774)
250/416             ZC 1786-1819,1826-36,B 1777-1806 ; copies A
                MARSH GIBBON UR (1828)                    Apply Ch. Sec
                NEWPORT PAGNELL UR (1660)
253-5               ZC 1790-1837,B 1790-1837 ; copies A
                OLNEY,Cowper Memorial UR (1700)           Apply Ch. Sec
                RAVENSTONE (1790-1868) no trace of records
                SHERINGTON UR (1782)                      Apply Ch. Sec
                STOKEC GOLDINGTON (1790-1971) no trace of records
                STOKENCHURCH   (1820) Now closed
1596                ZC 1830-36 ; copies A

                STOKE ROW/IPSDEN Now closed
1597                ZC 1818-23
                STONY STRATFORD EFCC (1808)
312/327             ZC 1816,1822-37,B 1824-37 ; copies A
                WENDOVER UR (1811)
258                 C 1819-36,B 1834-36 ; copies A
                WEST WYCOMBE (1805-55) no trace of records
                WHADDON IC (1829)                         Apply Ch.Sec
                WING (1805) Joined with Burcott  no trace of records
                WINGRAVE UR (1805)
260                 ZC 1817-37,B 1826-36 ; copies A
                WINSLOW (1816)   now closed
261                 ZC 1815-37 ; copies A + Members Roll 1824-96
                WOOBURN,Bethel (1773)   now closed
1798/320            C 1773-90,ZC 1791-1837,B 1783-1836 ; copies A
```

CAMBRIDGE & HUNTINGDON

```
                            C = Cambridge Record Office.
                            H = Huntingdon Record Office
RG4/
 -          BALSHAM (1833-1953) no trace of Registers
            BASSINGBOURN UR(1791)
2147                C 1820-37 ;  copies at C
            BOTTISHAM(1829-1968) no trace of Registers
            BURWELL UR(1692)
262                 C 1747-96,1819-36 ;  copies at C
            CAMBRIDGE,Emmanuel UR (1687)
2                   C 1739-80 ;  copies at C
            CAMBRIDGE,Hogg Hill (1696) now closed
3870/263            ZC 1688-1837 ;  copies at C
```

```
            CASTLE CAMPS UR (1817)
-                     Apply Church Sec.
            CHATTERIS UR(1838)
-                     C 1876+ at C
            DUXFORD UR (1794)
94                    C 1788-1836 ;  copies at C
            ELY IC (1785)
                      Apply Church Sec.
            EVERSDEN,GREAT (1689-1964)
169                   ZC 1787-1837,D 1811-1818
            FORDHAM EFCC (1818)
325                   ZC 1819-35,B 1825-32 ;  copies at C
            FOWLMERE UR (1780)
265/6                 ZC 1812-31,1833-37 ;  copies at C
            FULBOURN UR (1815)
150                   ZC 1816-37;   copies at C + C 1831-36
            GRANSDEN,GREAT (1662) became  Particular Bapt. 1733
                      Church Minutes 1694+ with Ch.Sec
            HINXTON (1836-1949).No trace of Registers
            HOUGHTON,Union Chapel now closed
                      M 1845-50,B 1841-1928 (H)
            KIMBOLTON (1692) now closed
                      Z 1743-59,1772-1819,C 1810-17 (H)
            KINGSTON UR (1842)    Apply Church Sec.
            LINTON UR (1689)
95                    ZC 1787-1839,B 1798-1837 ;  copies at C
            LITLINGTON CF (1815)
-                     Apply Church Sec.
            LITTLE SHELFORD UR (1823)
174                   C 1822-37;  copies at C
            MARCH,Station Road UR (1836)
-                     Apply Church Sec.
            MELBOURN UR (1694)
            NEWMARKET (viv 1850)  now closed, no trace
155/176               C 1800-37,B 1810-37 ;  copies at C
            ROYSTON,Old Meeting (1700)
218/326               C 1759-85,1822-50 ;   copies at C
            ROYSTON,New Meeting (1792)
96                    ZC 1830-37,B 1797-1837 ;  copies at C
            Both the above merged in 1922 but are now closed

            St IVES Free Church UR (1642)
678/8/74              C 1742-48,ZC 1748-1807 ; C 1742-1807,1814-29 (H)
            St NEOTS,High St UR (1669)
3247                  ZC 1802-35 ; C 1747-99,B 1837-70 (H)
            SAWSTON,High St UR (1811)
2022                  ZC 1803-37 ;  copies at C
            SOHAM (viv 1850) Now closed. No trace of Regs
-           THRIPLOW  (1780)  No known Regs,but later  merged  with
                                                         FOWLMERE

            WHITTLESEY UR (1813)
3541                  ZC 1810-37 ;  copies at C
            WISBECH   Cable Square UR (1818)
302                   ZC 1799-1837 ; copies at C; C 1784-1837(DWL)
            WISBECH,Gorefield (1836) No known records
            WRATTING,WEST   (1811)  No  known  records;merged  with
                      BOTTISHAM - see above
            YAXLEY now closed
                      C 1820-37 (H)
```

CHESHIRE

```
                         C = Chester Record Office
                         M = Manchester Local History Library
                         N = National Library of Wales
RG4/
          ALTRINCHAM,Bowdon Downs UR (1839)
  -               C 1840-1969,M 1846-63,1876-1972 (M)
          ASHTON-on-MERSEY,School Lane (viv 1850)
304               ZC 1799-1837;copies M
          BAWDON,Partington Chapel (1714-1951)
93                ZC 1815-37 ; C 1820-37 (M)
          BIRKENHEAD,Clifton Rd WI
  -               C 1842-54,B 1847 (N)
          CHESTER,Common Hall St (viv 1850)
  -               No trace of records
          CHESTER,Queen St (viv 1850)
160               ZC 1803-37 ; copies M
          CONGLETON,Mill St UR (1785)
178               ZC 1785-1837 ; C 1785-1837,B 1834-37 (M)
          DUKINFIELD,Providence (viv 1850)
179/81            ZC 1806-37,B 1807-37 ; copies M
          GATLEY UR (1778)
  -               C 1779-1944,B 1823-1950 (M)
          HATHERLOW UR (1645)
2091 & 2260/1     ZC 1785-1817,ZCB 1834-37,B 1793-1817 ;
                  C 1732-81,1785-1837,B 1793-1837 (M)
          HAZEL GROVE,Ebenezer UR (1827)
1103 & 182        ZC 1827-37,B 1828-37
          HULME,Zion,Stretford Rd
  -               C 1824-43 (M)
          HYDE,Union St UR (1814)
2150              ZC 1822-37 ; copies M
          KNUTSFORD & MOBBERLY (1826-1935)
172               ZC 1806-37 ; copies M
          MACCLESFIELD,Ebenezer,Townley St (1787) now closed
539               ZC 1785-1837,B 1789-1835 ; copies M
          MACCLESFIELD,Roe St (viv 1850)
540               ZC 1831-37 ; copies M ;
                  C 1785-1909,B 1789-1835 (C)
          MALPAS UR (1824)
185               ZC 1819-37 ; copies M
          MARPLE BRIDGE UR (1662)
943 & 505         ZC 1761-1840, B 1791-1837 ; copies M
          MIDDLEWICH,Queen St UR (1797)
186               ZC 1807-37, B 1817-25 ; copies M
          MINSHULL,Vernon UR (1806)
  -               C 1809-24 (C)
          MOBBERLY,Knolls  Green (1811-1961) Taken over by Pepper
          St (CF) ; early records may be with Knutsford.
          MOTTRAM.Hyde (1830) No trace ; no closed
          MOULTON (1833) viv 1915
  -               B 1837-41 (C)
          NANTWICH,Church Lane UR (1780)
188               ZC 1800-35 ; C 1813-55,B 1800-1905 (C)
                  C 1800-34 (M)
```

NORTHWICH UR (1708)
2094   ZC 1800-37 ; copies M
OVER,Nr Winsford UR (1814)   Apply Church Sec.
RUNCORN,Bethesda now Hallwood UR (1831)
-            CMB 1832-1945 (C)
RUNCORN,St Luke's(1830), merged with Bethesda c1835
SALE,Montague Rd UR (1805)   Apply Church Sec.
SANDBACH UR (1807)
217   ZC 1799-1837 ; copies M
STALYBRIDGE (1831-62)
2521 & 2398   C 1831-37,B 1834-37; copies M
STOCKPORT,Old Chapel (1672)
2023   C 1709-93 ; C 1709-1837 (M)
STOCKPORT,Tabernacle UR (1700)
420   C 1801-36,B 1807-37 ; copies M
      Churches merged c1956
STOCKPORT,Edward St now closed
7   ZC 1818-37 ; copies M
STOCKPORT Churchgate aka Orchard St (1788-1907)
421/2 & 521   ZC 1788-1837 ; C 1788-1811,1822-37 (M)
TINTWHISTLE,Nr Hyde UR (1688)
3533 & 2153   C 1747-1837 ; C 1747-1837,B 1798-1821 (M)
VICAR'S CROSS,Nr Chester UR (1772)   Apply Church Sec.
WALLESEY,Liscaid (1841) Now closed ; no trace
WHEELOCK,Nr Sandbach UR (1824)   Apply Church Sec.
WILMSLOW (viv 1850) now closed ; no trace
WINSFORD - see OVER

CORNWALL

                 T = Truro Record Office
RG4/
       ANTHONY,Bethel,Torpoint UR (1810)
440   C 1815-37 ; copies T
       CALLINGTON (1810) Sold to Weslyans 1835,no records
       CAWSAND,Garrett St CF (1793)
200   C 1810-37 ; copies T.Regs 1837+ with Ch.
                                                  Sec

       COVERACK (1820) now closed, no trace
       CREED (1784) now closed.Members' list 1820-21(T)
       FALMOUTH,Prince St (1662),Became Ind.c 1782.
4029   C 1783-1833, B 1808-37 ; copies T/SG
       FEOCK (1791) now closed, no trace of records
       FOWEY,Mount Zion (1797) now closed
4062   C 1798-1836 ; copies T/SG
       GERRANS (1822)Closed by 1850
2263   C 1826-36 ; copies SG
       GORRAN - see Mevagissey
       LANREATH,Ebenezer (1816) now closed
205   ZC 1816-37 ; copies T/SG
       LANTEGLOS,Fowey (1837) now closed, no trace of records
       LAUNCESTON,Castle St (1788-1956)
428   ZC 1777-1837 ; copies T/SG
       LEWANNICK,Polyphant (1817) closed by 1850, no trace
       LISKEARD(1701) Presbyterian from 1806, no trace of regs
       LOOE,WEST (1787)
207   C 1788-1837,B 1819-36 ; copies T/SG

```
                LOSTWITHIEL (1810-99)
567                     C 1812-37 ; copies T/SG
                MENHENIOT (1821) Closed by 1850, no trace of records
                MEVAGISSEY,Gorran UR(1776)
201                     C 1786-1837 ; copies T/SG
                NEWLYN (1812-60) No trace of records
                PENRHYN,New St (1795-1934)
434                     C 1806-37,B 1808-34 ; copies T/SG
                PENZANCE,Lower Meeting (1662-1968)
3119                    C 1791-1837,B 1806-37 ; copies T/SG
                PORTHALLOW (1830-77) No trace of records
                PORTHSCATHO - see Gerrans
                St AGNES (1779-1868)
2264                    C 1807-36 ; copies T/SG
                St AUSTELL,South St (1788) Now closed
568                     C 1789-1835 ; copies T/SG
                St BREOCK (1836) now closed,  no trace of records
                St COLUMB MAJOR,Bethesda (1794-1941)
437                     C 1795-1837 ; copies T/SG
                St COLUMB MINOR (1822) Now closed, no trace of records
                St ERTH,Praze (1820) Used in succession by Baptists,
                Presbyterians & Independents. No trace of records
                St GLUVIAS - see Penrhyn
                St ISSEY (1819-1969) No trace of records
                St IVES,Zion EFCC (1662) ; no early records
                St MAWES (1784) Now closed
109                     C 1798-1837 ; copies T/SG
                TORPOINT - see Anthony
                TREGONY CF (1824) Apply Church Sec.
                TRURO,Reiver St (1761-1933)
4681                    C 1789-1837 ; copies T/SG
                VERYAN.(1820) Now closed, no known records
                WADEBRIDGE (1835)Now closed, no known records
```

CUMBERLAND & WESTMORLAND

```
                        C = Carlisle Record Office
                        K = Kendal Record Office
RG4/
                ALSTON & GARRIGILL (Closed 1975)
72/208                  ZC 1764-1837,B 1782-1837 ; C 1763-1974,M 1843
                        -1942 ,B 1782-1942 (C)
                ASPATRIA (1814-1968)
835                     ZC 1821-37;  C 1853-1967,M 1860-1963,B 1860-
                        1966 (C)
                BOOTLE,Main St UR (1780)
                        C 1835+ ,B 1782+ with Church Sec.
                BRAMPTON (1818-1897) No trace of records
                CARLISLE,Lowther St & Annetwell CF (1786)
685                     ZC 1785-1836 ; C 1856-1868,M 1865-7, B 1859-
                        68 (C)
                COCKERMOUTH UR (1651)
490                     ZCB 1737-1837 ; C 1651-1908,MB 1848-1908 (C)
  -             KESWICK,Lake Road CF (1654) No early records
                KESWICK,Parkhead (1653) now closed
566/688                 C 1700-1836,B 1762-1802 ; CMB 1847-86 (C)
                KENDAL,Lowther St (1779-1929)  No trace of records
```

CUMBERLAND & WESTMORLAND (Contd)

KIRKBY LONSDALE (1815-1964)
2247   ZC 1813-36 ; C 1813-36 (K)
KIRKBY STEPHEN & WARCOP (1814-1946)
2248   C 1757-1836,B 1758-1822 ;   C 1844-1932,M 1868-
        78, B 1876-80 (K)
PENRITH,Ebenezer UR (1780)
4459   ZC 1815-37;C 1848-1908,M 1871-1909,B 1846-92(K)
PLUMBLAND (1844-1962) No trace of records
RAVENSTONEDALE UR (1662)
3970   ZCB 1775-1837
STAINTON (1698) Closed early 19c,no trace of records
TEMPLE SOWERBY (1662) Closed by 1850, no trace .
WARCOP - see Kirkby Stephen
WHITEHAVEN UR (1670)
2095 & 861   C 1789-1819,ZC 1789-1836,B 1823-33 ;
        C 1851-1968,M 1840-76,B 1855-76 (C)
WIGTON,Water St UR (1666)
689   ZC 1805-37,B 1835-37
WORKINGTON,Priestgate UR (1780)
Various   ZC 1745-1837

DERBYSHIRE

D = Derby County Record Office
M = Manchester Local History Library

RG4/

ALFRETON UR (1662) No early records
ASHBOURNE,Zion UR (1787)
        C 1787-1837,B 1808-37 (D)
BAKEWELL,Mill End (1788-1948)
492/3   ZC1799-1837 (Copies D/SG)
BARROW-on-TRENT - see Repton
BELPER & HEAGUE CF (1790)
692/3   ZC 1790-1836;C 1792-1836,B 1799-1891(D)
BOLSOVER & CLOWNE (1630-1980)
2155   C 1819-36; (Copies D/M)
BUXTON UR (1810) Apply Church Sec.
BUXWORTH CF (1826) Apply Church Sec.
CALOW UR (1837)
        B 1843-1984 (D)
CHARLESWORTH,St Mary's CF (1662)
703   ZC 1786-1837; C 1786-1841,M 1840-83, B 1848-
        1926 (D)
CHESTERFIELD, Soresby St (1788-1966)
495   ZC 1786-1837, B 1836 ; C 1776-1837 (D)
        C 1786-1837, B 1787-1837 (M)
CHINLEY CF (1662)
496   ZC 1682-1814, DB 1755-1814 ; C 1680-1837,
        B 1736-1837 (D)
CHINLEY CHAPEL,Glossop now closed
569   ZC 1807-37,B 1813-37
DERBY Brookside UR (1778)
696   C 1787-1837 ; C 1787-1975 (D)
DERBY Cox Bench (1828-1926) No trace of records
DRONFIELD, Salem UR (1812)
606   ZC 1806-36 ; C 1812-36,1926-74 (D)
FRITCHLEY CF (1840) Apply Church Sec.
GLOSSOP, Littlemoor (1811) Now closed
2096   C 1813-25 ; C 1812-83,M 1846-81,B 1825-1956
        (D) ; C 1813-37,B 1825-37 (M)

DERBYSHIRE (Contd)

```
                GLOSSOP,New Mills UR (1823)
503 & 116                 ZC 1829-37,B 1832-37
                GLOSSOP St Mary's now closed
                          C 1786-1837 (M)
                GREENBANK (1822-1965)
860                       ZC 1822-37; copies M
                HEAGUE - see Belper
                HEANOR (1790) linked with Marlpool after 1877
707,329/30                ZC 1791-1837,B 1822-37 ; copies D/M
                ILKESTON,Market St now Wharncliffe Rd UR (1772)
504,572 & 2157  ZC 1770-1837 ; copies D/M
                MARLPOOL UR (1801)  Apply Church Sec.
                MATLOCK BATH (1777-1947)
506                       ZC 1785-1836 ; copies D
                MELBOURNE, Penn Lane UR (1768)
1083                      ZC 1768-1837 ; copies D
                MIDDLETON & WARKSWORTH CF (1786)  Apply Church Sec.

                MIDDLETON-by-YOUGRAVE (1826) Now closed
                          C 1861+ (D)
                NEW MILLS (1823) Now closed
                          C 1829-37,B 1832-37 (D/M)
                PADFIELD,Temple St CF (1828)  Apply Church Sec.
                REPTON & BARROW UR (1780)
948                       ZC 1808-37 ;C 1814-37 (D/SG)
                RIDDINGS,Alfreton UR (1821)
2528                      ZC 1822-37 ; copies D/SG
                THORNSETT,Birchvale CF(1832)   Apply Church Sec.
                TIDESWELL UR (1830)   Apply Church Sec.
                TURNDITCH,Green Bank (1818-c1840)
                          C 1823-37 (D)
                WARKSWORTH - see Middleton
                WIRKSWORTH,Old Chapel (1700) Now closed
510                       ZC 1813-36 ; C 1813-36,1837-98,M 1868-97,
                            B 1866-74 (D/SG)
                YEAVELEY,Nethergreen Chapel (1814-1971)
456                       ZC 1815-24 ; C 1816-24 (D/SG)
```

DEVON

```
                E = Exeter Record Office
                P = Plymouth Record Office
RG4/
                APPLEDORE UR (1662)                    Apply Ch.Sec
                ASHBURTON,Great  Meeting(1665-1946).Originally  Presby
                -terian.  For  entries  1693-8 see Cullompton  Pres.Ch.
951                       C 1817-37 ; copies E/SG
                AXMINSTER,Chard St UR (1660)
511 & 841                 C 1786-1837 ; copies E/SG
                BARNSTAPLE,Cross St UR (1662)
Various                   C 1701-1837 ; copies E/SG) ; B 1840-58 (P)
                BEER CF (1700)
2401                      C 1788-1835 ; copies SG
                BEER ALSTON UR (1811)
514                       C 1813-37 ; copies E/SG
                BERRYNARBOR - see Ilfracombe
                BICKINGTON UR (1838)                   Apply Ch. Sec
                BIDEFORD UR (1660)
515                       C 1753-1837 ; copies E/SG ; C 1695-1927 (P)
```

DEVON (Contd)

```
            BOW Nr Crediton CF (1821)
578              C 1825-36 ; copies E/SG
            BRAUNTON UR (1662)
2402                ZC 1816-37 ; copies SG
            BRIXHAM Closed by 1855, no trace of records
            BUCKFASTLEIGH,Higher Chapel UR (1787)
1105                ZC 1787-1837 ; copies E/SG ; C 1787-1969 (P)
            CHUDLEIGH UR (1662) Presbyterian until 1794
518 & 3560       C 1711-1837 ; copies E/SG
            CHULMLEIGH CF (1633)
579                 ZC 1812-37 ; copies E/P/SG ; CMB 1848+ (P)
            COLYTON (1814-1962)
521              C 1815-37 ; copies E/P/SG
            COMBE MARTIN (1819)  viv 1850,now closed
3874             C 1829-36 ; copies E/P/SG
            CREDITON CF (1737)
522              C 1805-37,B 1804-37 ; copies E/SG
            CULLOMPTON (1831)   appeared closed by 1850
333              C 1831-37 ;  copies E/SG
            DARTMOUTH,Flavel   Memorial   UR   (1662)   Apply   Ch.Sec.
            DAWLISH (1814)  viv 1850 now closed
2277             C 1814-37 ; copies E/SG
            DEVONPORT,Mount St (1809)   now closed
962 & 581        C 1809-37,Z 1816-37 ; copies SG
            DEVONPORT, Mount Zion (1824)  now closed
580              C 1824-37 ; copies SG
            DEVONPORT,Princes St (1763) re-formed as Pilgrim UR
961 & 838        C 1763-1837 ; copy SG ; C 1817-1915 (P)
            DEVONPORT Salem later Wycliffe,now with Pilgrim UR
520 & 525        C 1826-37 ; copies SG
            DITTISHAM (1836-1967)
                 C 1828-1923,B 1844-1923 (P)
            EAST BUDLEIGH,Salem (1712)  now closed
2275 & 2532      C 1762-1837,B 1832-37 ; copies E/SG

            EXETER    Tabernacle(1770) Methodist until  1837  then
                      Independent
527              C 1776-1836 ; copies E/SG ; C 1788-1804 (DWL)
            EXETER,Grosvenor Chapel (1829-78) no trace of records
            EXETER,High St (1816) now closed
1086                ZC 1820-36 ; copies E/SG
            EXETER,Southernhay UR,(1795) originally in Castle Lane
1205/6 & 582     C 1798-1836,B 1800-36 ; copies E/SG
            EXMOUTH,Ebenezer (1806-1965)
2905             C 1809-37 ; copies E/SG
            EXMOUTH,Glenorchy UR (1777)
1209                ZCB 1751-1837 ; copy SG
            FRITHELSTOCK (1672-1715) no trace of records
            GALMPTON EFCC (1831) no registers before 1870
            GOODLEIGH (1830-1967)  no trace of records
            HARTLAND (1815-86)
529              C 1821-37 ; copies E/P/SG
            HAYES & HOLLACOMBE (1836-91)
                 C 1868-83,B 1870-83 (P)
            HOLSWORTHY (1828-30)
2098             C 1828-30 ; copies E/SG
            HONITON EFCC (1695) originally Presbyterian
various          C 1697-1857 ; copies E/P/SG
```

DEVON (Contd)

```
              ILFRACOMBE,Berrynarbor UR (1687)
1211 & 1081          C 1729-1837,B 1821-37 ; C 1729-1837 E/SG
              KERSWELL (1815) now closed
2278                 C 1816-32 ; copies E/P/SG
              KINGSBRIDGE,Ebenezer(1672-1924)       orig. Presbyterian.
                                               Independent from 1793
1212 & 443          C 1775-1837,B 1826-37 ; copies E/P Also C 1774-
                    1931,M 1837-97,B 1793-1897 (P)
              KINGSTEIGNTON,Zion UR (1816)
2534                 C 1808-35 ; copies E/P/SG
              LAPFORD CF Nr Crediton (1838)         Apply Ch. Sec
              LODDISWELL CF nr Kingsbridge (1808)   Apply Ch. Sec
              MUDDIFORD (viv 1850) Closed, no trace of records
              NEWTON ABBOTT,Salem UR (1662)
445                  C 1726-1837 ; copies E/SG
              NEWTON ABBOTT,Providence (1814)  now closed
1225                 C 1817-36 ; copies E/SG
              NORTHAM (1829-68)  no trace
              NORTH MOLTON (1825-68)  no trace
              NORTH TAWTON UR (1810)
452                  C 1812-36 ; copies E/SG
              OKEHAMPTON,Ebenezer UR (1799)
446/7 & 1214         C 1799-1836 ; copies E/SG
              OTTERY St MARY UR (1662)
2100                 ZCB 1785-1837 ;  C 1746-1837(E/SG) ;C  1746-
                     1938,M 1839-1937,B 1746-1955(P)
              PAIGNTON UR (1818)
2536                 C 1818-36,B 1826-36 ; copies E/SG
              PLYMOUTH,Pilgrim UR -see Devonport
              PLYMOUTH,Old Tabernacle - see Devonport

              PLYMOUTH,Norley Chapel (1797-1954)
1090                 C 1798-1837 ; copies E/P/SG
              PLYMOUTH Morice Square (1784)  now closed
RG8/10               ZC 1781-1806 ;  copies E/P/SG
              PLYMOUTH,Reheboth later Trinity, now closed(1833)
2101                 C 1833-37 ; copies E
              PLYMOUTH,Corpus Christi Stonehouse (1780) closed
120                  ZC 1786-1837 ; copy SG
              PLYMOUTH, Emma Place (1787) now closed
450                  C 1794-1836,B 1796-1836;C 1794-1836 (E) ;
                     C 1849+,M 1868+,B 1891+ (P)
              PLYMPTON,Lee Mill (1836-1967)
2538                 ZC 1836-37 ; copies E/P/SG
              PLYMTREE - see Kerswell
              POINT-in-VIEW - see Withycombe
              PUDDINGTON (1729-1968) No trace of records
              SANDFORD (viv 1850) No trace of records
              SEATON UR (1825)                      Apply Ch.Sec
              SHALDON Ebenezer (viv 1850)
1327                 ZC 1824-36 ; copies E/SG
              SIDBURY (1672-1972)
448                  C 1757-1836,B 1820-36 ; copies E/SG ;
                     C 1844-1961,M 1846-1957,B 1844-1972 (P)
              SIDMOUTH, Marsh Chapel UR (1813)
837                  C 1815-36 ; copies E/SG
              SOUTH BRENT CF (1819)                 Apply Ch.Sec
```

DEVON (Contd)

SOUTH MOLTON (1662) Now closed
449   C 1758-1837 ; copies E
        STOKENHAM,Ford Chapel (1662) Closed
834   ZCB 1772-1837 ; C 1772-1837 (E/SG)
        STOKE FLEMING (viv 1850) No trace of records
        TAVISTOCK,Brook St UR (1662)
451   ZC 1796-1836 ; C 1796-1911 (E/P/SG)
        TEIGNMOUTH,Zion UR (1790)
453   C 1804-36,B 1809-36; C 1809-36 (E/SG)
        TIVERTON UR (1660)
1764 & 2031   C 1766-1837 ; copies E/SG
        TOPSHAM CF (1804)
4473   C 1808-37 ; copies E/SG
        TORCROSS CF (1829) No records before 1883
        TORQUAY,Cary St (1824) now closed
454   C 1833-37 ; copies E/SG
        TORRINGTON UR (1662) no early records
        TOTNES,Fore St UR (1662)
1224   ZC 1794-1837 (E/SG) ; C 1793-1870,1876-9(P)
        UFFCULME & CULMSTOCK.(1663) Orig Presbyterian, now
                                                         closed
455   ZC 1790-1836 ; copies E/SG
        WESTLEIGH,Nr Tiverton UR (1824)   Apply Ch.Sec
        WITHYCOMBE RALEIGH (1777) Closed
1209   C 1779-1837,B 1784-1818 ; C 1779-1837 (E)
        WITHYCOMBE,Point-in-View (1826) now closed
2032   C 1829-37 ; copies E/SG

        WITHERIDGE Nr Tiverton CF(1839) no records before 1856
        WOLBOROUGH - see Newton Abbott

DORSET
                D= County Record Office,Dorchester
RG4/
-       ABBOTSBURY - see under Weymouth
        BEAMINSTER,East St CF (1688)
2403   ZC 1796-1836 ; copies D/SG
-       BERE REGIS EFCC (1662) o registers before 1936
        BLANDFORD FORUM UR (1662)
Various   ZC 1760-1809,C 1805-16,1818-36,B 1803-37 ;
                                           copies D/SG
        BROADWINSOR (1821) now closed, no trace of records
        BRIDPORT,New Meeting (1751) now closed
Various   C 1751-1836,D 1750-86 ; copies D
        BUCKLAND NEWTON CF (1839)   Apply Church Sec.
        CERNE ABBAS (1672) now closed
-               C 1863-74, M 1864-73,B 1869-70 (D)
        CHARMOUTH UR (1662)
2035   ZC 1779-94,1806-37,B 1817-37 ; Copies
                + C 1839-73,M 1840-66,B 1840-73 (D)
        CHICKERWELL,WEST (1816-1970) no trace of Registers
        CHRISTCHURCH UR (1660) now in Hampshire
Various   C 1780-1816,B 1786-94,1817-57; C 1780-1919,
                B 1786-94,1817-82 (D)
        CORFE CASTLE CF (1800)
458   ZC 1810-37
        CRIPPLESTYLE EFCC (1807)   Apply Church Sec.
        DORCHESTER,Dungate St UR (1662)
346   ZC 1788-1837

```
                HAMWORTHY (1804) now closed
54                   ZC 1833-37
-               HENSTRIDGE CF (1792)  no early records
                LYME REGIS,Coombe St(1666)  now closed
2269 & 462           C 1775-1836
-               LYTCHETT MINSTER UR (1770)          Apply Church Sec.
                MAIDEN NEWTON (1799-1932)  linked with Sydling
2410                 ZC 1833-35
                MARNHULL (1790) now closed, no trace of records
                MORECOMBELAKE UR (1831)
585                  ZC 1831-37
                PARKSTONE UR (1804)                 Apply Church Sec.
                POOLE,Skinner St UR (1662)
Various              ZC 1741-1837,B 1787-94,1802-37
                PORTLAND UR (1825)
2272                 ZC 1829-37
                SHAFTESBURY UR (1670)
348                  ZC 1799-1837
                SHERBORNE (1757) united with Presbyterians 1803;now UR
2413                 ZC 1785-1823 ; C 1824-37 (D)
                STALBRIDGE CF (1662)
586                  ZC 1810-37
-               STOKE ABBOTS UR (1837)              Apply Church Sec.
                STURMINSTER NEWTON (1818-1965) No trace of records
                SWANAGE UR (1705)
467 & 4460           ZC 1794-1837
                SYDLING,Hope Chapel (1775-1932)- see also Maiden Newton
349                  ZC 1811-35
                THREE CROSS,Nr Wimborne UR (1832)  Apply Church Sec.
                UPWEY UR (1802)                     Apply Church Sec.
                VENN UR (1816)                      Apply Church Sec.
                VERWOOD UR (1802)
-                    C 1816-37 (D)
                WAREHAM Meeting House Lane & West St(1672-1918)
Various              ZC 1740-1837 ; C 1740-1918,M 1857-1918,B 1824-
                     1918 (D)
                WEST LULWORTH (viv 1855) now closed, no trace of Regs
                WEYMOUTH ,Abbotsbury (1785) now closed
                     C 1877-1970 (CRO)
                WEYMOUTH,Chickerell IC (1816)    no early records
                WEYMOUTH,Gloucester St (1687)
                     C 1734-1836,M 1864-1881,B 1864-1869 (D)
                WEYMOUTH,Hope Chapel UR (1821)
                     C 1858-1924,M 1858-86,B 1858-86 (D)
                WEYMOUTH St Nicholas St (1687) Utd with Gloucester St
45 & 534             ZC 1734-1837
                WIMBORNE MINSTER UR (1670)
1884                 ZC 1768-1837,B 1791-1837
```

DURHAM

```
                D = Durham Record Office T = Tyne & Wear Record Office
RG4/
                BARNARD CASTLE,Gainford UR (1811)
4587                 CB 1806-37 ; C 1806-1908,M 1857-92,B 1855-1900(D)
                BISHOP AUCKLAND UR              Apply Church Sec.
                BISHOP WEARMOUTH, later Mallings Rig now closed
-                    ZC 1796-1894 (T)
                BISHOP WEARMOUTH,Bethel Chapel, now closed
588/914/2664         C 1811-36,B 1826-54 ; copies D
                BOLDON,EAST UR (1829) no registers before 1872
```

DURHAM (Contd)

```
                CHESTER-le-STREET Bethel UR (1814)
589                  ZC 1802-37 ; copies D
                COTHERSTONE CHAPEL(1748-1923) nr Barnard Castle
3150                 ZC 1749-1836
                DARLINGTON,Bethel UR (1806)
590                  ZC 1813-37 ; copies D
                DURHAM,Claypath UR (1778)
2265                 C 1751-1804,ZC 1778-1837,B 1830 ; ZB 1810-64(D)
2279 & 476
                FELLING,Zion (1830) now closed
1759                 ZC 1830-37 ; copies D
                GUISBOROUGH UR (1811)           Apply Church Sec.
                GREAT AYTON EFCC (1813)         Apply Church Sec.
                MIDDLETON-in-TEESDALE  Closed  by  1820,  no   trace
                MONKWEARMOUTH (1794) Later linked with Roker
479                  ZC 1788-1837
                SOUTH SHIELDS,Walker St , now closed
480                  ZC 1824-36; C 1824-74(D);C 1824-86(T)
                SOUTH SHIELDS,Mile End Rd, now closed
-                    ZC 1758-1936(T)
                STAINDROP (1827-1954)
592                  ZC 1806-37 ; copies D
                STANHOPE & WOLSINGHAM - see under DEVON
                     ZC 1813-28 (D)
                STOCKTON-on-TEES,Green Dragon Yard  now closed
RG8/1495             ZC 1789-1816,ZC 1821-36; copies D; C 1727-1817(T)
                SUNDERLAND,Corn Market now closed
1497/8               ZC 1717-1837; copies D
                SUNDERLAND,Roker UR (1794)
-                    CMB 1797-1976 (D)
                SUNDERLAND,Union Chapel (1817) No regs before 1881.
                WINLATON,Providence (1830) now closed
2417                 ZC 1830-37; copies D
                WOLSINGHAM - see Stanhope
```

ESSEX

```
                CH = Chelmsford Record Office ; CO = Colchester
                          S = Southend
RG4/
                ABBOTTS ROOTHING (1678-1910)
486                  ZC 1707-1828,1832-37; C 1838-1909(CH)
                AVELEY UR (1817)                    Apply Ch.Sec
                BADDOW,GREAT UR (1814)              Apply Ch.Sec
                BADDOW,LITTLE UR (1661)
2289 & 3875          ZC 1748-80,1799-1837; ZC 1799-1969(CH)
                BARKING,Upney Lanme UR (1782)
353/4                ZCDB 1804-37
                BATTLESBRIDGE CF (1836)             Apply Ch.Sec
                BILLERICAY UR (1672)
1499                 ZC 1754,1777-1837,B 1811-37
                BRAINTREE,Bocking End CF (1699)
various              ZC 1738-1857,DB 1779-1857
                BRAINTREE,London Road (1787)  now closed
1752                 ZC 1813-37,DB 1813-37
                BRENTWOOD,New Road UR (1799)
1752                 C 1707-1837,B 1800-37;C 1800-46,B 1800-45(CH)
                BRIGHTLINGSEA UR (1833)             Apply Ch.Sec
                BROXTED EFCC (1835)                 Apply Ch.Sec
                CANEWDON EFCC (1833)                Apply Ch.Sec
```

```
                CASTLE HEDINGHAM UR (1708)
487 & 1504           ZC 1775-1818,1822-37,B 1808 & 1813,1822-36
                CHELMSFORD,Baddow Rd (1672)  now closed
Various              C 1775-83,1786-1821,ZC 1794-1810 ;
                     C 1786-94,1812-39 (CH)
                CHELMSFORD,London Rd (1714-1970)
1766  & 2162         ZC 1759-1837,B 1818-36 ;  C 1759-1953,B 1818-
                     75(CH)
                     The above churches united in 1970 and are now UR
                     at New London Rd
                CHELMSFORD,Howe Green UR (1834)         Apply Ch.Sec
                CHIGWELL UR (1734)
355                  C 1806-37
                CHIPPING ONGAR - see Ongar
                CHISHALL (1688) Now closed
2906 & 612           ZC 1832-37
                CLAVERING UR (1682)
2666 & 833           ZC 1791-1837,M 1798,B 1794-1837
                COGGESHALL UR (1662)
Various              ZC 1752-1837,DB 1807-21,B 1821-37
                COLCHESTER,Harwich Rd UR(1845)        Apply Ch.Sec
                COLCHESTER,Christ Church UR(1843)
                     No regs before 1856
                COLCHESTER,Lion Walk UR(1642)
1508/9               ZC 1764-1837,B 1767-1837; C 1764-1948,M 1837-
                     38,B 1767-1903(CO)
                COLCHESTER,Shrub End UR (1843)         Apply Ch.Sec
                COLCHESTER,Stockwell Chapel (1662) now closed
357 & 2907           ZC 1784-1837
                DEDHAM (1738-1978)
1100 & 1511          C 1755-1823,ZC 1823-37 ;  C 1869-1906,1919-78
                     M 1875-1931,B 1883-1940(CO)

                DUNMOW UR (1662)
2852                 ZC 1733-69,1800-37;C 1733-71,1800-88 (CH)
                EPPING Lindsey St (1625) now closed
1512 & 800           ZC 1768-1837,B 1758-1817; C 1844-61,M 1851-62
                     B 1853-9 with gaps to 1943 (CH)
                FELSTED UR (1833)
2286                 ZC 1794-1837
                FINCHINGFIELD UR (1700)
598                  ZC 1815-37
                FORDHAM (1790-1968) later Countess of Huntingdon's
799                  ZC 1784-1837,B 1803-37
                GRAYS UR (1836)                         Apply Ch.Sec
                GREAT WAKERING,see under Wakering
                HALSTEAD,Old Meeting UR (1662)
2539 & 1513          ZC 1829-37,B 1792-1837 ; C 1761-1937 (CH)
                HALSTEAD,New Chapel (1662)
6                    ZC 1816-37,B 1832-33
                HARWICH,Bathside (1799-1941)
453/600              ZC 1783-1837
                HATFIELD HEATH UR (1662)
Various              C 1738-1837 ; C 1809-54, B 1830-53 (CH)
                HENHAM (1806- c1930)
2906                 ZC 1806-37 ; C 1806-35,1838-1903,1922-30,
                     M 1927 (3 entries) (CH)
                INGATESTONE UR (1812)
780                  ZC 1814-37 ; C 1813-63, B 1822-47 (CH)
                KELVEDON UR (1812)
796                  ZC 1811-37 ;  C 1811-1914,M 1865-1915,B 1852-
                     1915 (CH)
```

ESSEX (Contd)

```
            MALDON UR (1688)
1767                ZC 1776-1837,B 1809-37
            MANNINGTREE (1823-1924)
1379/80             ZC 1823-37,B 1823-25
            NAZEING EFCC (1795)  no early records
            NEWPORT UR (1682)
793                 ZC 1797-1837,B 1811-36 ;  C 1797-1966,B 1811-
                    1970 (CH)
            OCKENDON,SOUTH UR (1812)
4792                ZC  1815-37 ;  C 1815-29,M 1839-1928,B  1828-
                    1929 (CH)
            ONGAR UR (1662)
790/1 & 611         ZC 1764-1837,D 1766-80,B 1790-1837
            RIDGEWELL (1805) now closed
789                 C 1809-33
            ROCHFORD EFCC (1690)
788                 ZC 1767-8,1770-1837
            RODING,WHITE (1698) closed, no trace of records
            ROMFORD,Bethel (viv 1850)
1519                ZC 1812-18
            ROMFORD,Western Rd UR (1662)
  -                 C 1779-1854,B 1781-1855 (CH)
            ROOTHING - see Abbott Roothing


            ROYDON UR (1798)
  -                 C 1810-17,1851-1914,M 1897-1911,B 1851-
                    1910 (CH)
            SAFFRON WALDON,Abbey Lane UR (1665)
1520 & 387          ZC 1811-37,DB 1808-37 ; C 1799-1866,M 1839-65
                    B 1808-74 (CH)
            SOUTHEND,Cliff Town UR (1799)
782                 ZC 1830-37 ; C 1830-42 (S)
            SOUTHMINSTER UR (1800)
1804                ZC 1831-36
            STAMBOURNE CF (1662)
601 & 781           ZC 1815-37,C 1810-31, B 1814-37
            STANFORD RIVERS  now closed
123                 ZC 1823-36, B 1834 & 37
            STANSTED MOUNTFICHET UR ( 1698)
2541                ZC 1791-1837, ; C 1837-84 (CH)
            STANSTED ABBOTTS (1808)  now closed
  -                 C 1822-55,B 1822-41 (CH)
            STEBBING UR (1715)
1522                ZC  1793-1837  ;   C  1807-1960,M  1838-1933,
                    B 1816-26,1850-65 (CH)
            STEEPLE BUMSTEAD CF (1760)  no regs before 1836
            STOCK & INGATESTONE IC (1801)
780                 ZC 1814-37,B 1813-36
            TAKELY EFCC (1808)                    Apply Ch.Sec
            TERLING UR (1624)
1399                ZC 1750-56,1784-1837
            THAXTED UR (1662)
4031 & 4127         ZC 1771-1822,1827-37 ; Z 1844-48,ZC 1849-1956
                    M 1850-1956,DB 1835-1963 (CH)
            TIPTREE UR (1664)    no regs before 1850
            TOLLESBURY CF (1803)
2290                ZC 1817-37
            UPMINSTER,Upminster Hill (1801) now closed
1382                ZC 1801-37
            WAKERING,GREAT UR (1822)
  -                 C 1849-73,M 1851-1928.B 1880-85 (S)
```

```
613        WALTHAM,LITTLE UR (1790)
                   ZC 1803-21,C 1820-37,B 1823-37 ; C 1804-1933
                   M 1863-1918, B 1808-74 (CH)
           WALTON-on-NAZE UR (1837)                Apply Ch.Sec
           WEST  MERSEA  EFCC (1805)                Apply  Ch.Sec
```

GLOUCESTERSHIRE

```
                   B = Bristol Record Office
                   G = Gloucester Record Office
RG4/
           ADSETT (1838-1970) No trace of records
           AVENING,Upper Chapel Closed by 1845
774                ZC 1790-1837
           BERKELEY,Newport Meeting (1712) Now closed
2036               ZC 1822-36
           BLAKENEY Tabernacle (1823) now closed
620/1069           ZC 1823-37
       BRISTOL AREA
           BISHOPSWORTH (1828) Now closed, no trace of records
           BRISTOL,Bridge St (1671) Now closed
388                C 1714-1837 ; C 1800-68,M 1837-66 (B)
           BRISLINGTON UR (1796)             Apply Church Sec.
           Brunswick Chapel (1824-1964)
2686               ZC 1834-56,B 1837-56 ;  B+M 1837-1941(B)
           Castle Green Meeting UR (1670)
1359/1792          ZC 1784-1837 ; copies B
           CLIFTON DOWN (1662) merged with Bridge St
           CLUTTON (1834-viv 1850) No trace of records
           FELTON (1839) Now closed, no trace
           FRAMPTON COTTERELL Zion UR (1795)
4770               ZC 1801-37
           Highbury Chapel (1843) Closed, no trace
           Hope Chapel CF (1784) Early Regs destroyed per Ch.Sec.
           Newfoundland Rd,Gideon Chapel (1810-1930)
                   ZC 1822-37 (B)
           TIMSBURY CF (1825)                Apply Church Sec.
           TOTTERDOWN,Wycliffe (1843) Now closed, no trace
           UPTON CHEYNEY UR (1834) CMB 1861+ with church
           WESTERLEIGH,Zion (1835-1965 ?)
                   C 1838-1963,M 1837-1926(B)
           WICKWAR UR Lower Chapel UR (1836)
                   ZC 1818-36, B 1818-32 (B)

           CAM CF (1662)
                   C 1702-38,1776-88,1799-1970 (G); Copies with
                   Ch.Sec ; C 1702-1739,1776-1836 (SG)
           CERNEY,SOUTH CF (1824)            Apply Church Sec.
           CHALFORD,France Chapel (1782) Now closed
3767               ZC 1782-1837,B 1785-1837
           CHEDWORTH  (1750)  viv 1850  now closed
2103               ZC 1792-1836,B 1800-37
           CHELTENHAM,Highbury UR (1827)
2037               ZC 1828-37
           CHELTENHAM Independent Chapel (1809) now closed
3180               ZC 1810-37
           CHELTENHAM,Tewkesbury Rd (viv 1850) No trace
           CIRENCESTER,Wharfe Rd UR (1830)
2545               ZC 1817-37
           COLEFORD UR (1842)               Apply Church Sec.
           CROMHALL IC (1813)               Apply Church Sec.
           DIDMARTON CF (1843)              Apply Church Sec.
```

GLOUCESTERSHIRE (Contd)

DRAYCOTT (1820) Closed by 1845,no trace

DURSLEY,Corn Meeting
RG8/12b/12c   C 1702-1739,C 1775-90
RG4/   DURSLEY,Tabernacle UR (1710)
771 & 1387   ZCB 1754-1825,ZC 1825-37
        EBLEY IC (1797)
           Regs 1801-1948 (G)
        FAIRFORD,Crofts Chapel CF (1662)
3567   ZC 1787-1837, B 1787-1835
        FALFIELD (1813-1968) Reformed at STONE (1868-1931)
           No trace of records
        FRAMPTON COTTERELL - see under Bristol
        FRAMPTON-on-SEVERN (1776) Now closed
769   C 1777-1837,B 1778-96
        GLOUCESTER,Southgate St UR (1662)
768/616/1386   C 1748-1837,B 1786-1837
        HANHAM UR (1829)
        KINGSWOOD,Whitefield's Tabernacle UR (1739)
1375   ZC 1785-1837 ; ZC 1785-1837, B 1803-1915(B)
        LITTLEDEAN UR (1797)
766   C 1803-37,B 1821-37
        LONGBOROUGH (1838-1968) No trace of records
        LONGNEY CF (1838)   Apply Church Sec.
        MARSHFIELD Closed by 1845
4765   ZC 1806-33
        MITCHELDEAN UR (1662)
764   ZCB 1759-1837
        MORETON-in-MARSH (viv 1850)
763   ZC 1801-37
        NAILSWORTH,Forest Green CF (1662)
2102 & 3569   ZC 1732-1837 ; Regs 1775-1817 (G)
        NEWNHAM - see Blakeney
        NIBLEY,NORTH CF (1815)   C 1829-45 with Church Sec.
        NORTHLEACH - see Chedworth
        OLDLAND,Tabernacle UR (1811)   Apply Church Sec.
        PAINSWICK,Upper Chapel UR (1680)
866   ZC 1780-1837
        PITCHCOMBE (1804-1922)
1078   ZC 1801-37
        PUCKLECHURCH CF (1840)   Apply Church Sec.
        RANDWICK,Ebley Chapel later Countess of Huntingdon
762   ZC 1797-1837
        RODBOROUGH,Tabernacle UR (1760)
760   ZC 1762-1837,B 1823-37; copies G
        RUARDEAN (1789-1869)
1769   ZC 1795-1837,B 1802-37
        STONE (1868-1931) No trace, linked with Falfield
        STONEHOUSE (1812-1961)
1075   ZC 1824-30
        STROUD,Old Meeting (1711-1970))
Various   C 1712-1837, B 1720-29,1753-1837; Regs 1712-
                                   1970 (G)

GLOUCESTERSHIRE (Contd)

            STROUD,Bedford St CF (1837)   Apply Church Sec.
            STROUD,Ruscombe   CF   (1828) Apply   Church   Sec
            TETBURY,Lower Meeting (1710) Now closed
2105   C 1822-37

            TEWKESBURY,Upper Meeting (1707) now UR
757/8 & 1073   ZC 1752-1837
            THORNBURY (1720) Now closed
711   ZC 1796-1837,B 1816-36
            TIMSBURY,Zion CF - see Bristol
            TOTTERDOWN,Wycliffe - see Bristol
            ULEY,Union Chapel (1790-1963)
392   C 1793-1837
            UPTON CHEYNEY,Zion Chapel UR - see Bristol
            WESTERLEIGH,Zion Chapel - see Bristol
            WHITESHILL IC (1816),Winterbourne
2038   ZC 1824-34 ; later Regs with Church Sec.
            WICKWAR - see Bristol
            WOOTON-under-EDGE UR (1772)
395/6 & 2546   ZC 1772-1837,B 1772-83; Regs 1772-1880 (G)
            WOOTON,Kingswood CF (1662)
3044   ZC 1807-36,B 1822-36; Regs 1807-1959 (G)

HAMPSHIRE & ISLE of WIGHT

                        W = Winchester Record Office
                        P = Portsmouth Record Office
                        S = Southampton Record Office
    RG4/
            ALDERHOLT EFCC (1830)   Apply Church Sec.
            ALTON Normandy St UR (1662)
397   ZC 1788-1837,B 1834-35 ; Copies W
            ANDOVER,East St UR (1662)
709/10 & 2298   C 1739-90,ZC 1739-1837 ; C 1739-1837, B 1807
                  -1811 (W)
            BASINGSTOKE,London St UR (1663)
1071/2106   ZC 1739-1837 ; C 1739-1837 (W)
            BISHOPSTOKE (1820) Now closed
2039   ZC 1817-28 ; C 1817-28 (W/SG)
            BOTLEY (1806) No trace of records
715   ZC 1833-37 ; C 1833-37, B 1813-37 (W)
            BOURNEMOUTH East Howe UR (1834)   Apply Church Sec.
            BOURNEMOUTH Longham UR (1841)   Apply Church Sec.
            BOURNEMOUTH Pokesdown UR (1820)   Apply Church Sec.
            BOURNEMOUTH Throop UR (1828)   Apply Church Sec.
            CADNAM (1790-1964) No known records
            CHRISTCHURCH UR (1660)
399/717/1070   ZC 1780-1837,B 1817-37 ; C 1780-1837, B 1788
                  - 1837 (W)
            CRONDALL (closed 1969)
718   ZC 1792-1836 ; C 1792-1836 (W)
            ELING,Totton Chapel (1811)
1885   ZC 1818-37
            EMSWORTH Nile St UR (1808)
2166   ZC 1817-37 ; C 1817-37 (W)
            FAREHAM UR (1691)   Apply Church Sec.
            FINCHDEAN UR (1830)   Apply Church Sec.

```
         FORDINGBRIDGE (viv 1850)
719              ZC 1795-1837 ; C 1795-1837 (W/SG)
         FROGHAM EFCC (1820)                Apply Church Sec.
         GOSPORT,High St UR formerly North Quay Chapel (1663)
1391/2108        C 1691-1837 ; copies W
         HAVANT UR (1710)
720              ZC 1779-1837 ; C 1779-1837 (W)
         HAYLING ISLAND UR (1811)           Apply Church Sec.
         HOOK (1816) Now closed but linked with Odiham
         HYTHE UR (1839)                    Apply Church Sec.
         LYMINGTON,Old Town Chapel UR (1700)
721/2300/1       C 1753-1837 ; C 1753-1836,1847-1921,M 1848-
                 85, B 1847-1903 (W)
         LYMINGTON East End Chapel UR (1810) Apply Church Sec.
         NEW ALRESFORD (1825-61)
1072             ZC 1832-37 ; C 1832-37 (W)
         OAKHANGER (1820) Closed 1930s ? No trace of records
         ODIHAM, High St (1662-1958)
723              C 1795-1837,B 1833-37 ; Copies W
         PETERSFIELD UR (1722)
724/2855         ZC 1794-1837,B 1810 & 1825 ; C 1799-1837 (W)
         PORTSMOUTH,Buckland UR (1835)
                 CMB 1878+ (W)
         PORTSEA,Orange St (1754-1936)
867              ZC 1785-1837 ; ZC 1785-1893 (P)
         RINGWOOD,Lower Meeting UR (1781)
725              ZC 1808-37 ; C 1790-1964,M 1856-76,B 1820-71
                                                        (W/SG)
         ROMSEY & BRAISHFIELD UR (1662)
1364/5           ZC 1758-1836,B 1784-1834 ; copies W
         ROWLANDS CASTLE,Providence Chapel UR (1797)
716              ZC 1799-1837 ; copies W
         SOPLEY Closed 1942
656/7            ZC 1829-37,B 1829-37 ; copies W
         SOUTHAMPTON Above Bar ,Now St Andrew's UR (1662)
610/624/658      ZC 1783-1823,C 1823-37,B 1821-37 ; C 1674-1837
                 B 1726-1837 (W) ; C 1783-1837,B 1821-37 (S/SG)
                 C 1836-1915,B 1837-1851,1896-1913 (S)
         SOUTHAMPTON Peartree Green UR (1808) Apply Church Sec.
         STOCKBRIDGE,Salem Chapel (1815) now closed
625              ZC 1815-36 ; C 1815-36 (W)
         STUCKTON EFCC (1827)               Apply Church Sec.
         TADLEY UR (1662)
2305             ZC 1788-1835
         WINCHESTER,Jewry St UR (1662)
20/762/3562      ZC 1716-1837 ; C 1716-1837 (W)


ISLE of WIGHT
                 N = Newport Record Office

         BRADING UR (1832)
                 B 1847-1974 (N)
         COWES,EAST (1829)
1107             ZC 1829-37 ; copies W ;C 1828-1917(N)
         COWES,WEST Union Rd EFCC (1805)
608              ZC 1804-37,B 1821-34 ;  copies W/N  ; C 1837-
                 1908 (N)
         NEWPORT CF St James St (1662)
                 C 1784-1837 (W) ; C 1802-37 (N)
         NEWPORT Node Hill, now closed
                 C 1802-37 (W)
```

```
            PORCHFIELD Now closed
                   C 1848-1908,B 1848-1978 (N)
            RYDE,George St Chapel UR (1802)
1373               C 1817-37 ; copies W/N ;C 1837-1909 (N)
            VENTNOR UR (1834)                    Apply Church Sec.
            WHITCHURCH     (1658-1919)   No    trace   of    records.
```

HEREFORD & WORCESTER

```
                        H = Hereford Record Office
                        W = Worcester Record Office
RG4/
            BROADWAY UR (1792)
2960               ZC 1801-37; copies W
            BROMSGROVE,Chapel Lane (1693)   now closed
2135  & 3481       ZC 1739-1837,  B 1772-1837;  C  1739-68,1770-
                   1837,Z 1832-37,B 1772-88,1834-37 (W)
            BROMSGROVE Worcester St UR (1832)
2734               ZC 1785-1804,  Z 1804-36; Z 1785-1836,C 1788-
                   1804 (W)
            BROMYARD (viv 1845)
3561               ZC 1696-1836, B 1784-7,1808-31; copies H/SG
            DUDLEY King St UR (1792)
2851               ZC 1803-37 ; copies W/SG
            EVESHAM (viv 1845 now closed) no trace of records
            HEREFORD Eign Brook UR (1662)
3572               ZC 1690-1836, B 1827-35; copies H/SG
            HUNTINGTON UR (1804)
                   C 1900-06,M 1907-65 (H) ;
            KIDDERMINSTER Old Meeting , now Baxter UR (1662)
3374 & 2899/90     C 1727-1837
            KIDDERMINSTER Park St (1774-1925)  no trace of Regs
            LANGLEY GREEN UR (1790)
                   Earliest records commence 1851 with Ch.Sec.
            LEDBURY (1607-1969)
729                C 1785-1837; copies H/SG
            LEIGH SINTON (1835-1963)  no trace of records
            LEINTWARDINE (1835) viv 1871  no trace of records
            LEOMINSTER Broad St (1829-35)
2423               ZC 1829-34; copies H/SG
            LYE UR (1809)  no early records
            MALVERN,GREAT (1826-72)  no trace of records
            MALVERN LINK UR (1835)
2989               ZC 1828-37
            OMBERSLEY (1820) viv 1855, no trace
            PEMBRIDGE (1820-1937)
1371               ZC 1822-36; copies H/SG
            REDDITCH UR (1818)
4487               ZC 1824-37, B 1827-37;ZC 1823-37,B 1827-37(W)
            ROSS  Kyrle St (1662) orig.Presbyterian,  now Worcester
                                                              Rd UR
733/6              CB 1732-1837; copies H/SG
            ROSS,Congregational Chapel now closed,joined Kyrle St
                   C 1734-1802,1825-1863 (H)
            STOURBRIDGE,High St UR (1672)
4130               ZC 1792-1837;  copies SG;Z 17899-1837,C 1790-
                   1837 (W)
            SUCKLEY (1821-1963)  no trace of records
            WHITCHURCH Doward Chapel UR (1816)
737                C 1820-33; copies H/SG
            WORCESTER Angel St, now Albany Terrace UR (1687)
Various            ZC 1699-1759,1780-95,1810-37,B 1783-93,1815-
                   37; C 1699-1955,M 1838-40,B 1783-1899 (W)
```

WYEBRIDGE,Hereford (1707) now closed
Some christenings with Eignbrook records(H)

HERTFORDSHIRE

H = Hertford County Record Office

RG4/

ASHWELL High St UR (1767)
738   ZC 1797-1837,B 1798-1836
BALDOCK UR (1826)   Apply Church Sec.
BARKWAY EFCC (1783)
1649   ZC 1812-37
BARLEY (1841) viv 1845   no trace of records
BARNET Wood St UR (1669)
C 1824+,MB 1853+ (H)
BERKHAMSTED UR (1780)
40/41 & 660   ZC 1787-1837,B 1793 ; copies SG
BISHOP'S STORTFORD,Water Lane UR (1662)
Various   ZC 1748-1837,B 1805-36 ; C 1837-1860 (H)
BRAUGHING EFCC (1691)
3574   C 1804-36
BRICKET WOOD,Spicer St now closed,no trace of records
BROXBOURNE - see Hoddesdon
BUNTINGFORD UR (1674)
740   ZC 1810-36,B 1818-25
BUSHEY UR (1809)
1646   ZC 1812-37 ; C 1814-1935,M 1839-1935,B 1838-
1940 (H)
CHESHUNT,Meeting House,now High St UR (1782)
741/2 & 868   ZC 1783-1837
GUILDEN MORDEN CF (1841)   Apply Church Sec.
HADHAM,LITTLE EFCC (1800)
745   ZC 1804-37,B 1833-36
HARPENDEN UR (1818)
2112   ZC 1819-21
HATFIELD,Christ Church UR (1823)   Apply Church Sec.
HEMEL HEMPSTEAD,Box Lane (1600-1967)
4475/2040/2549   ZC 1790-1837,B 1792
HEMEL HEMPSTEAD,Pope's Lane (1818-1967)
665   C 1824-37,B 1837
HERTFORD,Cowbridge Chapel UR (1660)
2552   ZC 1785-1800,1821-37 ; C 1769-1809,1825+,
M 1848+,B 1848+ (H)
HERTFORD HEATH (1830-1970) no trace of records
HITCHIN UR (1690)
743/744   ZC 1771-1837,B 1786-1836
HODDESDON UR (1781) renamed Broxbourne c.1980
1366   ZC 1818-37
KING'S LANGLEY,Zion Chapel now closed
2307   ZC 1834-37
PUCKERIDGE EFCC (1819)   Apply Church Sec.
REDBOURN (1806) now closed
746   ZC 1813-36
REDHILL (1662-1968) no trace of records
ROYSTON,Kneesworth St now closed
C 1794-1829,CMB 1842- ,(H)
St ALBAN'S,Spier St EFCC (1797)
623   ZC 1796-1837
SANDON UR (1662)   Apply Church Sec.

```
                SAWBRIDGEWORTH EFCC
                    ZC 1817-37
                THERFIELD EFCC (1836)              Apply Church Sec.
                WALKERN UR (1810)
750                 ZC 1814-37
                WARE Old Meeting UR (1662)
673                 ZC 1786-1836,B 1783-1834 ; C 1778-1786 (H)
                WARE,New Chapel(1811)  now closed
1374                ZC 1811-37
                The above chapels merged in 1859 and now worship in the
                High Street.
                WATFORD,Gilead,formerly Ebenezer (1814) now closed
675                 ZC 1808-1830 ; C 1811-1813,CMB 1869+ (H)
                WELWYN,Bethel (1792) now closed
3181                ZC 1793-1837
                WHEATHAMSTEAD Brewhouse Hill UR (1812)
                    CB 1822+,M 1844+ (H)
                WHITWELL (1800) now closed
2308                C 1835,B 1834
                WORMLEY IC (1834)                  Apply Church Sec.
```

KENT

```
                F = Folkestone Archives
                M = Maidstone Record Office
                R = Ramsgate Archives
RG4/
            ASHFORD UR/M ,Bank St (1662)              Apply Ch.Sec
            BENENDEN (1835) now closed, no trace of records
            BIRCHINGTON,Ebenezer (1814) now closed
1682            C 1814-37
            BROADSTAIRS UR (1601)
                Registers commence 1876
            BROMLEY, Bethel UR Widmore Rd (1788)
26              ZC 1788-1832
            CANTERBURY,Guildhall St (1646-1942)
Various         C 1646-1837
            CANTERBURY,Union Chapel, now St Andrew's UR  (1645)
872             ZC 1792-1837
            CHATHAM,Ebenezer (1662)
680/3952        ZC 1774-1823,1823-37
            CRANBROOK CF (1710)
31              ZC 1786-1837
            DARTFORD,Lowfield St, formerly Zion Chapel (1790)
918             ZC 1797-1837
            DARTFORD,West Hill UR, formerly C of Hunt (1818)
1368            ZC 1820-33
            DEAL UR (1662)
RG4/1003/874    CB 1681-1802,ZCB 1802-37; CB 1802-43,M 1838-
                46,(F) copies SG
            DOVER,High St UR (1644)
1376            C 1710-16,B 1732-44
            EDENBRIDGE (1801) now closed
923             ZC 1806-37
            FAVERSHAM,Partridge Lane UR (1789)
879             ZC 1790-1837,B 1794
            FOLKESTONE,Tontine St (1797) now closed, no trace
            FOUR ELMS EFCC (1831)                  Apply Ch.Sec
```

```
                GRAVESEND,Princes St (1662) now St Paul's UR
1372/1110/1111      C 1762-1855,B 1761-1854;C 1837-1884,M 1856-68
                    B 1837-1869 (M)
                GREENHITHE (1817)  now closed, no trace
                GREENWICH,Greenwich Rd Chapel now closed
Various             C 1777-1857,B 1809-54
                GREENWICH,Maze Hill Chapel now closed
Various             ZC 1811-37,B 1825
                HERNE BAY,Union Chapel UR,Mortimer St (1822)
933                 ZC 1826-36,B 1828-34
                HYTHE,Ebenezer Chapel (1814 viv 1850) now closed
1009                ZC 1816-37
                IDEN GREEN CF (1833)                    Apply Ch.Sec
                ISLE of GRAIN UR (1823)                 Apply Ch.Sec
                LENHAM,Ebenezer UR (1784)
934                 ZC 1779-1837
                LITTLEBOURNE UR (1814)                  Apply Ch.Sec
                LYDD  now closed
2310                ZC 1814-37
                MAIDSTONE, (1746) Re-formed 1965, now Week St UR
1101/3575/15        C 1749-1837,B 1815-26
                MARDEN EFCC (1804)
1680                ZC 1812-36
                MILTON UR,nr Sittingbourne (1792)
3954                ZC 1807-36; copies M
                MINSTER-in-SHEPPEY CF (1801)
3576                ZC 1833-37
                NEWNHAM (1816)  now closed
1681                ZC 1825-37
                QUEENBOROUGH,Bethel Chapel (1796 viv 1850)
1011                C 1797-1836
                RAMSGATE,Ebenezer UR (1662)
Various             C 1695-1837,B 1788-1837 ; ZC 1695-1785,B 1837
                    -1919 (R)
                RAMSGATE,Zion Chapel(1816-32) replaced by Hardres St UM
1982                ZC 1817-32
                SANDWICH,Cornmarket UR (1644)
938/1183            ZC 1690-1837
                SHEERNESS,Union St (1725) now Hope St UR
627/1185            ZC 1791-1834,Z 1805-34; CB 1859+,M 1862+ (M)
                SNODLAND UR (1822)
                    ZC 1836-1867,1883-1907 (SG)
                STAPLEHURST UR (1647)
2553/1980           C 1797-1836
                STROOD,Zoar Chapel (1796) now closed
1189                ZC 1791-1836
                SUTTON VALENCE,Ebenezer (1794)  now closed
1012                ZC1795-1836; copies M/SG; C 1838-1975 (M)
                TONBRIDGE UR (1751)
14/2114             C 1752-1837 ; copies Tonbridge Library
                TUNBRIDGE WELLS,Mount Zion Chaepl (1830) now closed
1981                ZC 1830-37
                WELLING UR (1825)                       Apply Ch.Sec
                WESTERHAM EFCC (1838)                   Apply Ch.Sec
                WHITSTABLE UR (1808)                    Apply Ch.Sec
                WINGHAM (1825)  now closed
2555                ZC 1819-37
```

P = County Record Office Preston
M = Manchester Local History Library
N = National Library of Wales
R = Rochdale Archives Office

RG4/

ACCRINGTON viv 1850 now closed, no trace
AFFETSIDE Nr Bury CF (1825)   Apply Ch.Sec.
ASHTON-in-MAKERFIELD CF (1829)
1999   ZC 1819-36 ; copies P & M
ASHTON-under-LYNE,Albion St UR (1816)
1996   ZC 1815-36 ; copies M ; ZC 1815-51 (P)
BAMFORD UR (1801)
2168/2429   ZC 1800-36,B 1826-36; copies M/P;C 1801-1943,
              M 1826-1913,B 1826-1942 (R)
BARROW Nr Whalley UR (1662)
              No early records
BELMONT Nr Bolton (1814) Now closed
              Misc. entries 1840 + (P)
BELTHORN UR (1818)
              ZC 1824+ with Church ; C 1824-1963 (M/P/SG)
BISPHAM UR (1834)   Apply Ch.Sec.
BLACKBURN,Chapel St UR (1778)
1018/19   C 1777-1837,Z 1806-37,B 1785-1837 ; C 1777-
              1837 (M & P) ; MIs 1810+(P)
BLACKLEY Chapel Lane now closed
              C 1752-66 (P), copies (M)
BLACKPOOL,Bethesda CF (1809)
              Misc. entries (P)
BLATCHINWORTH & CALDERBROOK (1825-1879)
2786   ZC 1825-37 ; copies M & P ; Z 1808-37 (R)
BOLTON,Mawdesley St (1808-1962)
4365   C 1819-37 ; C 1831-1860 (P)
BOLTON,Duke's Alley now St George's Rd UR (1752)
1462   C 1785-1818 ; copies M & P
BRETHERTON ,Ebenezer CF (1819)
1117   ZC 1819-37 ; copies M & P
BRIERFIELD,Providence (1836) now closed
              No regs before 1850 ; P holds 1850-1947 MIs
BURNLEY,Bethesda UR (1807)
628   ZC 1807-37; copies M & P; P holds 1817-51 MIs
BURNLEY,Tabernacle viv 1850 now closed, no trace
BURY Bethel,Henry St IC (1820)
4472/806   ZC 1803-37 ; copies P & M
BURY,New Rd UR (1665)
2431 & 1976   ZC 1782-1837,B 1818-23 ; C 1782-1837 (P)
              C 1796-1837 (M & SG)
BURY,Walmersley Park Chapel (viv 1850 now closed)
4032   ZC 1803-37
CALDERBROOK - see Blatchinworth
CHAIGLEY,Walkerfold (1807-1952)
1030   ZC 1807-30 ; C 1807-37 P & M; OR 1807-84 (P)
CHIPPING,Hesketh Lane IC (1838)
              C 1807-1884 (P)

CHORLEY,George St (1836-1958) no trace of Regs
CHORLEY Hollinshead UR (1780)
812   ZC 1792-1837,B 1793-1836 ; copies P &
CHORLTON-on-MEDLOCK,Rusholme Rd now closed
813   ZC 1826-37 ; copies M & P
CHORLTON-on-MEDLOCK,Cavendish St now closed
        C 1789-1969 (M)
CLITHEROE,Wellgate UR (1817)
629   ZC 1814-37 ; copies P
CLOUGHFOOT(1840) closed, no known records
COCKERHAM,Forton Chapel UR (1707)
1032   ZC 1785-1837,B 1792-3 ; copies M & P
COLNE,Dockwray Sq UR (1807)
815   ZC 1810-37 ; copies M & P ; OR 1811+ with Ch.
DARWEN, OVER, Pole Lane UR (1793)
1017   C 1793-1830; C 1750-1837,B 1793-1820 (M/P/SG)
        MIs 1794-1887 (P)
DARWEN,OVER, Lower Chapel UR (1687)
1020/882/2001   C 1751-1791,ZC 1785-1837,B 1785-89,1819-21 ;
        C 1751-1837,(M & P) B 1793-1820 (M) ; MIs
        1729-1859 (P)

DARWEN,OVER,Belgrave (f Ebenezer Chapel) UR (1687)
125/1201   Z 1736-1837,C 1820-31,B 1819-21;C1736-1837 (P)
DENTON,Hope Chapel UR (1836)   Apply Ch.Sec.
ECCLES,Patricroft Chapel UR (1796)
819   C 1799-1837,B 1820-37 ; copies M & P
ECCLES Pendlebury (1814-1913) - see also Swinton
1337   C 1819-37; copies M/P
EDGEWORTH (1814-1963)
1038   C 1807-37 ; copies M/P ; OR 1869-1928(P)
EGERTON UR (1662) No records before 1899
ELSWICK,Memorial UR (1649)
2314/5 & 1039   C 1717-85,ZC 1785-1809,1832-36,B 1836-37 ;
        copies M ; C 1717-1837 (P)
FARNWORTH,Halshaw Moor (1809) now closed
820   ZC 1809-37; copies M/P
FORTON - see Cockerham
GARSTANG UR (1777)
66   ZCB 1784-1837 ; CB 1784-1837(M/P)
GOLBORNE CF (1830)   Apply Ch.Sec.
GOOSENARGH,Inglewhite Chapel now closed
128   ZC 1828-37; copies M/P
HALSHAW MOOR - see Farnworth
HARWOOD,GREAT UR (1841)   Apply Ch.Sec.
HASLINGDEN,Dearden Gate UR (1785)
822   ZC 1785-1837; copies M/P
HEATON MERSEY CF (1825)   Apply Ch.Sec.
HINDLEY,St Paul's Chapel (1812) now closed
828   C 1811-36 ; copies M/P
HINDLEY Bridgcroft (1838-1916) no trace of records
HOLCOMBE BROOK - see Tottington

```
            HORWICH Lee Lane UR (1770)
1472             ZC 1765-1836; copies M/P; OR 1840-1894(P)
            HORWICH New Chapel UR (1716)
1473/3847/3892   C 1751-85,ZC 1785-1837,B 1826-35; copies M/P
            INGLEWHITE CF (1819)
                 C 1828-37 (P) OR 1828+ at Church
            KIRKDALE,Claremont Chapel now closed
1887             ZC 1831-37; copies M/P
            KIRKHAM,Zion UR (1805)
2116             ZC 1810-37; copies M/P
            LANCASTER,High St now closed
various          C 1760-1857,B 1776-1837; copies M
            LEIGH,Bethesda EFCC (1807)
1476             ZC 1810-37; copies M
            LITTLEBOROUGH,Summit Chapel (1825) now closed
                 OR 1853-1972 (P)   00
            LIVERPOOL Bethesda, Duncan St, viv 1850 now closed
1204             ZC 1801-37; copies M/P
            LIVERPOOL Great Cross Hall St (closed 1895)
52 & 939         ZC 1802-37; copies M/P; C 1802-54 (N)
            LIVERPOOL Great George St (1777) now closed
1478/3358        ZC 1795,1803-37;  OR 1811-1966 (P);  C  1812-
                 37(M)
            LIVERPOOL Greenland St viv 1850, now closed
971              ZC 1818-37; C 1830-37 M/P
            LIVERPOOL Bethesda, Hotham St (1802-1904)
                 OR 1802-1904 (P)
            LIVERPOOL Hanover Chapel, Mill St now closed
                 OR 1830-1846 (P)
            LIVERPOOL Newington Chapel, Renshaw St (closed 1871)
1045 & 1484      ZC 1776-1837,B 1787-1808,1819-37 ; copies M/P
                 OR 1837-53 (P)
            MANCHESTER Cannon St later Grosvenor St (1753) closed
3127 & 3135      ZC 1760-1837,B 1786-88; copies M/P;C 1837-62
            MANCHESTER Jackson's Lane now Chorlton Rd UR (1756) (M)
3581             ZC 1824-37; copies M/P
            MANCHESTER Mosley St (viv 1850 now closed)
2694             ZC 1792-1837; copies M/P/SG
            MANCHESTER  Chapel Lane (viv 1850) - see Blackley
            MANCHESTER Roby Chapel UR (1756)        Apply Ch.Sec.
            MANCHESTER Stretford, Chester Rd (1817) closed
                 OR 1832-1850 (P)
            MANCHESTER Swinton (1820-1967) joined with Eccles &
                                                 Pendlebury
            MIDDLETON Providence Chapel (1822) no trace
            MOSSLEY Micklehurst UR (1824)          Apply Ch.Sec.
            NEWTON-le-WILLOWS (1842)  no trace
            NORTH MEOLS (1806-1900)
977              ZC 1806-36; copies P/M
            OLDHAM Greenacres CF (1662)
978/9            ZC 1763-1836,B 1828-37; copies C 1763-1836 M/P
```

```
                OLDHAM Hope St CF (1825)
2173 & 3583          C 1825-37,B 1828-37; copies M/P
                OLDHAM Providence Chapel (1829-1967)
1056                 ZC 1828-37; copies M/P
                OLDHAM Queen St (viv 1850)
980                  ZC 1829-37 ; copies M/P

                OLDHAM Delph CF (1745)
                     C 1780-1851,B 1783-1851 (M); OR with Church
                OLDHAM Dobcross Chapel CF (1839)
                     No records before 1871
                OLDHAM Ebenezer Chapel Upper Mill CF (1807)
                                                Apply Ch.Sec.
                OLDHAM Heyside UR (1800)
                     No records before 1850
                OLDHAM Radcliffe St CF (1807)        Apply Ch.Sec.
                OLDHAM Union St UR (1816)            Apply Ch.Sec.
                ORMSKIRK UR (1828)
                     OR 1848-76 (P)
                ORRELL (1824) now closed, no trace
                PENDLEBURY - see ECCLES
                PILKINGTON Stand Lane now closed
985                  ZC 1792-1837; copies M/P
                PRESCOT Ebenezer Chapel UR (1756)
1148                 ZC 1799-1837; copies M/P
                POULTON-le-FYLDE UR (1808)           Apply Ch.Sec.
                PREESALL Bethel Chapel UR (1835)     Apply Ch.Sec.
                PRESTON Cannon St (viv 1850)  now closed
1693                 C 1790-1809,1821-37,B 1790-1821; copies M/P
                PRESTON Church St now Grimshaw St UR (1808)
987                  ZC 1803-37,B 1808-37 ; copies M/P
                RAINFORD,Higher Lane UR (1702)
988                  C 1746-1837,B 1746-1836; copies M/P/SG
                     MIs 1727-1973 (P)
                RAMSBOTTOM Park Chapel UR (1798)
                     No records before 1883
                ROCHDALE  Smallbridge UR (1822)      Apply Ch.Sec.
                ROCHDALE  Providence now closed
1153                 ZC 1808-36; copies M/P/R
                St HELEN'S New Chapel UR (1688)
various              C 1734-69,1771-1837,B 1812-37; copies M/P/SG
                SALFORD  New Windsor Chapel now closed.
1773/1618/9     C 1798-1837,B 1800-37; copies M/P
                SOUTHPORT East Bank Lane UR (1807)
1064                 ZC 1812,1823-37 ; C 1824-37 M/P
                STALYBRIDGE  Bethel Chapel closed 1956
                     OR C 1789-1837 (P) ;copy M ; OR 1838-1956 (M)
                STALYBRIDGE Melbourne CF (1831)
                     C 1834-37 (M)
                TOCKHOLES UR (1662)
                     ORZC 1778+,B 1818-70 with Ch.Sec.
                TODMORDEN (1841-1967) No known records
```

```
                TOTTINGTON   Dundee Chapel closed 1901
1705                    ZC 1802-17; copy M ; C 1699-1837 (P)
                TOXTETH PARK UR (1833)
2440                    ZC 1833-36; copies M/P
                TURTON   Egerton Chapel, now closed
1123                    ZC 1784-1837; copies 1811-37 M/P
                ULVERSTON Soutergate Chapel (1777-1968)
                       No trace of records
                WALKERFOLD - see Chaigley
                WARRINGTON   Cairo St (formerly Sankey St) closed 1970
1623                    ZC 1724-1837,B 1788-1837; C 1724-1969 M/P/SG
                WARRINGTON   Stepney Chapel viv 1850 now closed
1167                    ZC 1798-1837; copies M/P/SG
                WESTHOUGHTON   Bethel Chapel UR (1827)
1293                    C 1826-37; copies M/P
                WHITWORTH   Hallford UR (1698)
                       C 1752-1925,B 1790-1967 (R)
                WIGAN Boar's Head Chapel (1751-1967)
2444                    C 1782-1823
                WIGAN Hope Chapel UR (1802)
                       C 1802-37 P/M
                WIGAN St Paul's, Standishgate (1775) now closed
1171/1294              ZC 1777-1837,B 1786-1837; copies M/P
                WORSLEY combined with Pendlebury
                       C 1819-37 (M)
```

LEICESTER & RUTLAND

```
                       L = Leicestershire Record Office
RG4/
                ASHBY-de-la-ZOUCH,Kilwardly St UR (1662)
360                    ZC 1812-37; copies L
                BURBAGE CF (1817)                Apply Ch.Sec.
                EARL SHILTON UR (1810)
888                    ZC 1774-1836; ZC 1810-38 (L)
                GREAT EASTON including Caldicott now closed
                       C 1827-1880 (L)
                HALLATON (1813) now closed, no trace
                HINCKLEY,Chapel St UR (1662)
1297                   ZC 1767-1836; copies L
                KETTON,Chapel Lane CF (1829)
1891                   ZC 1823-36; copies L
                KIBWORTH Now closed
                       C 1806-43,1867-1953,B 1867-1953 (L)
                KIBWORTH HARCOURT ,Leicester Rd CF (1662)
1441                   ZC 1785-1837 ; ZC 1806-37 (L)
                LEICESTER,Bond St Chapel (1801-1966)
3188/1338             ZC 1801-36,B 1824-36 ; copies L/SG
                       CMB 1858-1920 (L)
                LEICESTER Gallowtree Gate (1824-1921)
2338/2448             ZC 1817-37,B 1824-37;copies L/SG;B 1838-61(L)
                LEICESTER Salem Chapel,Free School Lane (1818)
1300                   ZC 1804-33 ;ZC 1813-33 (L);
                       Z 1805-33,C 1813-33 (SG)
                LOUGHBOROUGH Barden Park UR (1662)
1629                   ZC 1799-1837; ZC 1826-37 (L)
                LUTTERWORTH Old Meeting (1689)
Various                ZC 1733-1832 ; copies L
```

	LUTTERWORTH George St UR
2563	ZC 1823-37; copies L
	George St & Old Meeting subsequently merged
	MARKET BOSWORTH (1799)
1305	C 1812-22 ; C 1813-22,1825-36 (L)
	MARKET HARBOROUGH CF (1662)
Various	ZC 1753-1837,B 1787-1808,1813-37 ; copies L
	MELTON MOWBRAY UR (1821)
2564/2119	ZC 1822-37,B 1824-36; ZC 1822-1971,M 1837-1909,B 1824-36 (L)
	NARBOROUGH CF (1662)
2450/1774/1306	ZC 1790-1837; ZC 1755-1907,M 1861-1919, B 1797-1900 (L)
	NEWTON BURGOLAND,Hepzibah Chapel CF (1790)
2327	C 1803-35; copies L
	OAKHAM,Barr Gate CF (1662)
1812	ZC 1759-1837; Z 1759-1783,ZC 1786-1837 (L)
	SHEEPY MAGNA (1816) Now closed
	ZC 1825-36 (L)
	ULLESTHORPE,Claybrook CF (1805)
2328/1308/9	ZC 1805-36,B 1820-31; copies L
	UPPINGHAM,Ebenezer Chapel CF (1700)
1604	ZC 1785-1836; copies L
	WIGSTON MAGNA UR (1666)
1310/11	ZC 1773-1837,B 1805-37; copies L + later deps

LINCOLNSHIRE

	L = Lincoln County Record Office
	H = Huntingdon Record Office
RG4/	
	ALFORD IC (1795)
2451	ZCB 1822-36,M 1830,B 1834-36; ZCB 1826-36(L)
	BARNETBY viv 1845, no trace of records
	BARROW-on-HUMBER viv 1850, now closed
RG8/29	C 1808-34; copies L
	BARTON-on-HUMBER Providence Chapel UR (1789)
RG4/1928;RG8/29	ZC 1789-1836; ZC 1789-1856 (L)
	BOSTON,Grove St Chapel (1819-1956)
1929	ZC 1815-37; copies L/SG
	BRIGG,Wrawby St (1718) now closed
1313/2567	ZC 1792-1837; copies L/SG
	CADNEY viv 1850, no trace
	CAISTOR viv 1850, no trace
	CROWLAND viv 1850, no trace
	CROWLE (1760-1916) no trace
	GAINSBOROUGH, Caskgate St UR (1776), now in Church St
1315/1637	ZC 1798-1814,C 1814-36; C 1707-1836 (L)
	GRANTHAM St Peter's Hill (1819),now Avenue Rd UR
	no early records
	GRIMSBY viv 1850, no trace
	HELPRINGHAM viv 1850, no trace
	HOLBEACH closed 1965
	CMB 1889-1899,C 1918-65 (L)
	HORNCASTLE UR (1820)
1640	ZC 1820-37; ZC 1822-37 (L)
	KIRTON-in-HOLLAND (1802-1939)
1642	ZC 1802-37; C 1832-36,,CMB 1877-1909 (L)

LINCOLN,Newland UR
CMB 1891-1905 with L
LINCOLN,High St (1811-1936)
1643   C 1811-37; C 1819-36 (L)
LINCOLN,Zion Ch.- later Countess of Huntingdon (1774)
1696   ZC 1774-1833,B 1785-1833; copies L
LITTLE GONERBY now closed but linked with Grantham
ZC 1825-36 (L)
LONG SUTTON (1818) now closed
1932   ZC 1813-37; ZC 1820-37 (L)
LOUTH,Cannon St (1821) now closed
1933   C 1816-37; ZC 1820-37 (L)
MARKET RASEN (1821-1932) now closed
1935   C 1823-36; ZC 1823-36
PINCHBECK,Money Bridge Chapel (1787-1974)
1321   C 1785-1837,B 1822-36; C 1785-1836 (L)
SLEAFORD,Henland & Zion (1776) now Southgate UR
1322   ZC 1789-1837; copies L
SLEAFORD,Providence Chapel now closed
1319   ZC 1812-40; copies L
SPALDING,Pinchbeck St UR (1819)   Apply Ch.Sec
SPILSBY,Zion Chapel (1795-1892)
1116   ZC 1810-21; ZC 1811-21,C 1811-47 (L)
STAMFORD,Star Lane Chapel UR (1662)
3588/1941   C 1797-1837; copies L/H
SUTTON - see Long Sutton
TALLINGTON viv 1850, no trace
WELTON-le-MARSH viv 1850, no trace
WINTERINGHAM viv 1850, no trace
WITHAM,SOUTH viv 1850, no trace
WRAWBY,Middleton Lane (1798-1875)
1323   ZC 1817-38; copies L

LONDON, NORTH (Inc. MIDDLESEX)

G = Greater London Record Office
GL = Guildhall Library
RG4/
ACTON, Churchfield St UR (1817)   Apply Ch.Sec.
ALDERMANBURY,Founder's Hall Chapel closed by 1850
4215/6,4292,4216   ZC 1730-1837,C 1755-85
ALDERSGATE St,Hare Court Chapel   closed by 1850
4368   ZC 1820-37
ALDERSGATE,Jewin St,moved to Harrow 1905
4273   ZC 1789-1837
BARBICAN CHAPEL,Cripplegate   now closed
4218-20,4370   ZC 1776-1822,1829-57
BARTHOLOMEW CHAPEL & WOODBRIDGE CHAPEL now closed
4371   ZC 1827-37
BETHNAL GREEN,Cambridge Heath Rd (1662) now closed
4177/8,4137   ZC 1704-1836, C 1845-58; C 1704-55(SG)
BETHNAL GREEN,Sidney St Chapel   now closed
RG8/31/32   ZC 1846-1880
BETHNAL GREEN,Virginian Chapel   now closed
RG8/33   ZC 1825-37
BRENTFORD,Albany Chapel UR (1693)
370   ZC 1831-37; C 1694-1865,B 1786-1856 (G);
C 1831-37 (GL/SG)

```
                BROAD ST, Bartholomew's Close & Pinner's Hall, closed
4134/5,4226         C 1740-79,ZC 1774-1824
                BROAD ST,New Meeting House            now closed
4376                ZC 1727-1837
                BROMPTON ROW,Trevor Chapel,Arthur St (viv 1850)
4378                ZC 1816-37
                BUNHILL ROW                closed by 1850
4479                C 1793-99
                BURY ST,St Mary Axe            closed by 1850
4185                ZC 1781-1832
                CAMDEN TOWN,Ebenezer (viv 1850)
4384                ZC 1817-37
                CAREY ST,WC2 New Court Chapel (viv 1850)
4228/30,4484        C 1707-57,1759-86,ZC 1786-1837 ;
                    C 1707-1837 (SG)
                CHELSEA,Cook's Ground        closed by 1850
4179,4386           ZC 1772-1781,1786-1827
                CHELSEA,Union Chapel Sloane St closed by 1850
4385                C 1835-36
                CITY ROAD ,The Tabernacle  (viv 1850)
4262/4523           ZC 1768-1840
                CLAPTON,New Chapel UR Lower Clapton Rd (1804)
4144                ZC 1816-37
                CLAPTON,Upper Chapel UR Upper Clapton Rd (1812)
                    Apply Ch.Sec.
                COMMERCIAL ROAD,Wycliffe Chapel closed by 1850
Various             ZC 1785-1837,B 1798-1836
                CROWN St SOHO,Wardour Chapel (viv 1850)
4301                ZC 1819-37
                DALSTON,Middleton Rd (1662-viv 1850)
                    No known records
                EALING GREEN UR (1800)  No early records

                EDGWARE,Grove Rd (1834) now closed
1334                ZC 1834-37,B 1835; copies G/SG
                EDMONTON,Edmonton & Tottenham Chapels UR
371/2               ZC 1830-37,B 1821-37; C 1802-20,B 1792-1826
                    (G); C 1818-37,B 1821-36 GL/SG
                EDMONTON,Winchmore Hill UR (1750)
2458                ZC 1819-37,B 1831-2; C 1822-37,B 1831-2
                    GL/SG
                ENFIELD,Chase Side UR (1780)
1128 & RG8/79       ZC 1808-36; copies SG; C 1790-1840 (GL)
                ENFIELD,Highway now closed
1130                C 1830-38; copies GL/SG
                FINCHLEY,EAST (1815) no known records
                FINSBURY CIRCUS,Finsbury Chapel now closed
                    C 1824-89,M 1838-64 (G)
                FISH St HILL,King's Weigh House  closed by 1850
Various             ZC 1738-75,1779-1837
                GRAVEL LANE,St George in the East
4304/4155/6         ZC 1704-1837,B 1737-1837
                GRAYS INN RD,Providence Chapel appears closed by 1850
4240/4242           ZC 1784-1835
                HABERDASHERS HALL,Staining Lane closed by 1850
4243                ZC 1785-1825; C 1832-38 (GL)
                HACKNEY,Old Gravel Pit Meeting House now closed
4336                ZC 1802-37
```

```
          HACKNEY,St Thomas' Square now closed
Various         C 1765-1812,ZC 1787-91,1814-37,B 1787-1837
also RG8/41-51
          HACKNEY,Well St (1823) now closed
4398            ZC 1837
          HAMMERSMITH,Ebenezer Chapel now closed
374             ZC 1773-1833,B 1786-87; copies SG
          HAMMERSMITH,George Yard, formerly Presbyterian
2203/3595/375   ZC 1758-1837; copies SG
          HARROW,Hindes Rd UR, originally in Jewin St Aldersgate
                Church Minutes 1827+ with church
          HIGHGATE,Salem Chapel now closed
1131            ZC 1785-1836; C 1785-1836 GL/SG
          HOLBORN,City Temple UR (1640)
4407/4507       C 1798-1815,1818-19
& RG8 52-66
          HOLBORN,Fetter Lane Chapel now closed
                C 1730-1896 (G)
          HOLBORN,Trinity Chapel,Leather Lane now closed
4502            ZC 1835-37
          HOLLOWAY,Camden Rd UR (1802)
4309            ZC 1815-37
          HOUNSLOW,Ship lane UR (1824)
1946            ZC 1827-36; C 1827-36,B 1829-33 (GL/SG)
          HOXTON,Academy Chapel now closed
4530            ZC 1800-36
          HOXTON,Pavement Chapel now closed but viv 1888
4340            ZC 1778-1825; C 1845-88,M 1851-78
          ICKENHAM UR,Middx (1831)            Apply Ch.Sec.

          ISLINGTON,Maberley Chapel,Ball's Pond Rd now closed
4270            ZC 1826-37
          ISLINGTON,Barnsbury Chapel now closed but viv 1850
4341            ZC 1835-37
          ISLINGTON,Lower St Chapel now Harecourt UR (1648)
4191            ZC 1769-1837
          ISLINGTON,Union Chapel CF (1799)
4189            ZC 1805-37
          ISLINGTON,Upper St Chapel now closed
4190/4342       ZC 1804-37
          KENSINGTON,Kensington Chapel UR (1793)
                No records before 1882
          KENSINGTON,Hornton St Chapel now closed
1947            ZC 1825-37; copies GL/SG
          KENTISH TOWN,Kelley St Chapel CF (1807) Apply Ch.Sec.
          KINGSLAND now closed
4344            C 1795-1848,B 1826-43
          LEYTON,Langthorne Rd UR (1660) no early records
          LEYTONSTONE,New Court UR (1827)        Apply Ch.Sec.
          LIMEHOUSE,Coverdale Chapel- see also Stepney CF
4159            C 1849-57
          MARSHALL St,Regent St,W1  now closed
4194            C 1823-37
          MAYFAIR MARKET,Ebenezer Chapel now closed
4279/4347       ZC 1804-37,1830-37
          MARYLEBONE,Blandford St now closed
                C 1782-1820 (G) copies GL
          MILE END, Latimer Chapel (1827)  now closed
4526            ZC 1825-37
          MILE END, New Town Chapel  now closed
Various         B 1815-54
```

```
              MILES LANE, Cannon St,City now closed
4199                ZC 1786-1795
              MILL HILL, now Union Church UR
377                 ZC 1784-1830; C 1819-25 GL/SG; see also
                    Southwark Park St
              MILL HILL SCHOOL Chapel (1807)
376                 ZC 1831-37; C 1831-37 GL/SG
              NEW TOWN, Tonbridge Chapel viv 1850 now closed
4534                ZC 1811-37
              ORANGE ST EFCC, Leicester Square (1693)
4280                ZC 1831-37
              PADDINGTON, Paddington Chapel UR (1813)
4348                ZC 1813-36
              PELL St, St George in the East now closed
4251                ZC 1736-1829
              PENTONVILLE, Claremont Chapel now closed
4282                ZC 1819-37
              PIMLICO, Buckingham Chapel,Palace St now closed
Various             ZC 1795-1804,1820-37,B 1794-1804,1819-46
              PLAISTOW, Barking Rd UR (1807)
2540                ZC 1833-37
              PONDERS END UR (1745)
2459/60             ZC 1785-1800,1805-36; Copies GL/SG
              POPLAR, Millwall Chapel   now closed
4167                ZC 1823-36
              POPLAR, Union Chapel      now closed
4166                ZC 1812-37
              POULTRY Chapel, formerly in Camomile St EC3- closed
4410/4207           ZC 1702-53,1781-1837
              POYLE, Poyle Rd UR (1814) joined with Methodists 1987
2568/1132           ZC 1820-37,B 1826-35; copies GL/SG
              PUTNEY now closed
                    C 1817-34 (GL)
              RATCLIFFE, Queen St Chapel now closed
4311/4284           ZC 1693-1837,B 1822
              RATCLIFFE, Rose Lane - united with Queen St 1834
4259                ZC 1784-1834,B 1786-1833
              REGENT'S PARK, Albany Chapel (viv 1850) now closed
4397                ZC 1835-37
              ROBERTS St Chapel, Grosvenor Square  now closed
4169                C 1827-36
              SHADWELL,Ebenezer Chapel  now closed
4411                ZC 1824-37,B 1822-37
              SHOREDITCH, Gloucester Chapel now closed
4510/4413/4315      ZC 1814-37,B 1820-37
& RG8/69
              SHOREDITCH, Honeywell Mount Chapel now closed
4257/4412/4508      ZC 1783-1837; C 1837-54 (G)
              SOHO, Little Chapel St   now closed
4346                ZC 1796-1836
              SPITALFIELDS, Whites Row Chapel now closed
4210/4537           ZC 1756-1837; C 1756-1908 (G)
              STAINES, Kingston Rd EFCC (1789)
2461/1948           ZC 1785-1837; copies GL/SG
              STANMORE - see under Edgware
              STEPNEY, Bull Lane now Stepney Way UR (1644)
4414                ZC 1644-1837,M 1646-1677,B 1780-1837 ;
                    M 1646-77 (SG)
              STEPNEY, Coverdale & Ebenezer CF Bigland St (1785)
RG8/20              ZC 1796-1820
              STEPNEY, Cannon St Rd    merged with Bigland St
                    C 1792-1810 (G)
```

STEPNEY, Latimer Chapel CF,Ernest St SE1 (1672)
All records destroyed in WW 2
STEPNEY, New Road now closed
C 1811-37 (G)
STOKE NEWINGTON, Abrey Chapel Church St (1662); closed
4172/3   ZC 1785-1836,B 1838-52
STRATFORD, Brickfields Chapel (1662) now closed
1068/2421/2   C 1774-1838,B 1784-1854
SUNBURY-on-THAMES (1817-1968)
No known records
TOTTENHAM COURT RD, Whitfield's Tabernacle (1756)
4200   ZC 1805-40; B 1790-1838 (G)
TOTTERIDGE - see Whetstone
TWICKENHAM, First Cross Rd (1802) now closed
No known records
UXBRIDGE, Providence Chapel
Various   ZC 1789-1809,1812-37,B 1812-37,1847-55;
CB copies GL/SG
WALTHAMSTOW, Marsh St UR (1672)
1102   ZC 1788-1837
WHETSTONE (from 1827 Totteridge)
C 1788-1837,B 1800-37 (GL/SG)
WINCHMORE HILL UR - see under Edmonton

LONDON, SOUTH   includes parts of pre-1974 Surrey & Kent
GL = Guildhall Library
G = Greater London Record Office
GM = Guildford Muniments
RG4/

BERMONDSEY, Jamaica Row (1665-1907)
4260/4221   C 1781-1836
BERMONDSEY, Ebenezer Chapel,Neckinger Rd (now closed)
4372/4222/4136 C 1818-36,B 1811-53
BRIXTON, Trinity CF (1828)   Apply Ch.Sec
BRIXTON, Holland Rd Chapel (now closed)
4377   ZC 1824-37
CAMBERWELL, Albany Chapel (1801-93)
4383   C 1836-41
CAMBERWELL, Grove Chapel UR (1774)
4382   ZC 1819-37
CAMBERWELL, Mansion House Chapel (1780) now closed
4381   ZC 1801-37
CAMBERWELL, Marlborough Chapel closed by 1850
4227   ZC 1833-37
CLAPHAM, Nags Head Lane now Grafton Square UR (1645)
3100   ZC 1824-37; copies GL/GM/SG
CLAPHAM, Park Road now closed
C 1819-37 (GL)
DEPTFORD, Ebenezer,King St now closed
4334   ZC 1811-34
DEPTFORD, High St,formerly Butt's Lane (1660-1970)
4498/4302   ZC 1755-1836,B 1785-1837 ;C 1785-1969,B 1785-
1936,Lewisham Library
DEPTFORD, Medway Place now closed
4185   ZC 1781-1832
DEPTFORD, New Cross Chapel now closed
4389   ZC 1820-36
DEPTFORD, St Paul's & Woolwich now closed
4233   ZC 1806-32
GREENWICH, Mauritius Rd SE10 (1786) now closed,no
trace
HORSLEY DOWN, Union Chapel Parish St now closed
4187 & RG8/72-3 ZC 1824-37

LONDON - South (Contd)
```
              KENNINGTON, Esher St Chapel (1833)  now closed
4402                   ZC 1834-35,ZC 1833-37
              KENNINGTON, Carlisle Chapel (1811)  now closed
4401                   C 1817-34
              KENNINGTON, Vauxhall Chapel,Kennington Lane  now closed
4274/4158              ZC 1817-35,B 1817-37
              LAMBETH, Christchurch & Upton UR/B (1783) -    see also
                                           Southwark,Surrey Chapel
                       ZC1835-92 at Minet Library; ZC 1835-50(G/SG)
              LAMBETH, Lower Norwood   now closed
                       CB 1821-37 (GL)
              LAMBETH, Union Chapel Brixton Hill (1829)  now closed
1897/2585        Z 1833-37,C 1834-37,B 1834-37; copies GL/GM/SG
              LEWISHAM, High St UR (1797)          Apply Ch.Sec
              MITCHAM - see Surrey
              NEWINGTON, Locks Field Chapel (1790)  now closed
4202/3,4368            ZC 1804-37,B 1791-1801,B 1804-37
              NEWINGTON, Beresford Chapel (1818-41)
4363                   ZC 1821-37
              NORWOOD,WEST, Lower Chapel Rd UR (1806)
2888/1745        Z 1818-37,C 1821-37,DB 1821-37; copies GL/GM/SG
              PECKHAM, Hanover Chapel now Bellendon Rd UR (1687)
4281                   C 1801-37
              PUTNEY, Platt Chapel (1808)  now closed
2889               Z 1816-18,1827-34,C 1817-19,1827-34;
                                           Copies GL/GM/SG
              ROTHERHITHE, Southwark Park (1792)  no trace of records
              SOUTHWARK,  Colliers'Rents, White St (1730) later moved
                                     to New Kent Rd, now closed
4145/4181/4267         C 1751-1836,B 1767-1836
              SOUTHWARK, Globe Alley (1592)  now closed
4154                   ZC 1756-98
              SOUTHWARK, Goat Yard Passage (1652) later Tooley St
                       Z 1656-1712,M 1660-1700,D 1676-1712;
                       copies of M 1660-1700 (GL/GM/SG)
              SOUTHWARK, Guildford St  now closed
4335                   ZC 1804-37
              SOUTHWARK, Horsley Down Chapel  now closed
4181/RG8.72-3          ZC 1824-37
              SOUTHWARK,Park St Chapel  now closed
                       C 1784-1830 (GL)
              SOUTHWARK, St George's Chapel London Rd (1792) closed
4278                   ZC 1791-1825
              SOUTHWARK,  Surrey Chapel (1783) C of Huntingdon's from
                 1876 - re-founded as Christchurch.See under Lambeth
Various                ZC 1787-1837
              SOUTHWARK,  Union St Chapel  now closed
4356/4360              ZC 1823-5,B 1738-1837
              STOCKWELL, New Chapel UR (1796)
4326/4327              ZC 1802-37,B 1818-37
              STREATHAM HILL UR (1829)
1897/2585              CB 1834-37
              TOOTING, Rookstone Rd UR (1688)
2732               ZC 1786-1836,B 1786-1834; C 1786-1836 GL/GM/SG
              WALWORTH - see Newington
              WANDSWORTH, East Hill UR (1809)
2215                   ZC 1811-37,B 1815-37; copies GL/GM/SG
              WOOLWICH, Salem Chapel Powis St now closed
1990/1113              C 1796-1837,B 1824-36
              WOOLWICH, Union Chapel  now closed
1014/3479              ZC 1819-33, B 1819-37
```

N = County Record Office Norwich

RG4/

ALBURGH (1825-1968) no known records
ALBY (1651)   no known records
BLONORTON   Deeds from c1756 held at N
BRADFIELD (1657-1969)
1251   ZC 1692-1836,B 1828-34; see also Southrepps
BRISTON EFCC (1777)
1344   ZCB 1786-1840; Z 1694-1854(N) inc.Guestwick
BURNHAM WESTGATE (1807-1926)
639   ZC 1810-21,1824-35 ; Members List 1809-87 (N)
CREAKE,SOUTH (1783) now closed
1968   C 1786-1835,B 1795-1828; C 1846-60,M 1858-60,
        B 1837-1946 (N)
DENTON UR (1655)
1345   ZCB 1806-37; C 1765-1805,B 1778-1805(N)
DEREHAM,Cowper Memorial EFCC (1772) see also Mattishall
1259   ZC 1772-1837 ; copies N
DISS UR (1837)   Apply Ch.Sec.
EDGFIELD (1653) now closed, no known records
ELMHAM,NORTH (1824-1960) no trace of records
FAKENHAM (1819-1962)
3599/1253   ZC 1821-37
GUESTWICK (1652) see Briston
HAPTON (1645) Originally Presbyterian
1255   ZC 1792-1830,B 1808-34
HARLESTON,Mendham Chapel UR (1706)
        C 1807-37(N)
HINGHAM EFCC (1836)   Apply Ch.Sec.
KING'S LYNN,Broad St (1754-1962)
2467   C 1745-77,ZC 1777-1837
LONG STRATTON - see under Stratton
MATTISHALL UR (1650)
2572/1259/1956 ZC 1785-98,1828-37; copies N/SG ; see also Dereham
NORWICH,Old Meeting CF (1642)
1753/1260/653   ZC 1714-1837,B 1751-1837; C 1642-81,1768-1839 (N)
NORWICH,Princes St UR (1819)
1962   ZC 1812-37,B 1824-33 ; copies N
NORWICH,Tabernacle (1753-1879) no known records
OULTON (1725)
1262   ZC 1725-1837; copies N
RUNHAM (1642) now closed, no known records
SHIPDAM UR (1833)
1264   ZC 1833-37; copies N
SOUTHREPPS - see Bradfield
STRATTON CF (1825)
1568   ZC 1825-37 ; C 1837+,B 1845+ (N)
THETFORD,Earles St UR (1816)
365   C 1822-35,B 1820-36; copies N
TROWSE (1820-1956) no known records
TUNSTEAD (1652) no known records but linked with
                                        Bradfield
WALSHAM,NORTH CF (1657)
                              Apply Ch.Sec.

NORTHAMPTONSHIRE

N = County Record Office Northampton
H = Huntingdon Record Office

RG4/

        ASHLEY & WILBARSTON (1793-1963)
889   ZC 1781-1836; ZC 1790-1837 (N)
        BRACKLEY UR (1836) Earliest Regs 1852+ at Church
        BRIGSTOCK UR (1778)
2790/1269   ZC 1782-1837; copies N
        BYFIELD UR (1828)
2860   ZC 1827-36 ; copies N
        CHARLTON (viv 1850) no trace of records
        COLD ASHBY (c1750) closed by 1850, no trace
        CORBY UR (1824)   Apply Ch.Sec.
        COTTINGHAM (1808) now closed, no trace
        CREATON,High St UR (1670)
1271   ZC 1782-1837; copies N
        CRICK UR (1820)
2475   ZC 1824-36 ; ZC 1825-36 (N)
        DAVENTRY,Sheaf St UR (1672)
75   ZC 1746-1837 ; copies N
        DODDINGTON ,GREAT (1819) closed by 1950, no trace
        EVERDON (1811) closed by 1950, no trace
        FLORE - see Weedon
        GEDDINGTON UR (1672) no pre-1850 records
        HADDON,EAST (1812) now closed, no trace
        KETTERING,Toller UR Gold St (1662)
Various   ZC 1714-1837,B 1786-1837; ZC 1714-1873,B 1786
                -1837 (N); C 1714-1836,B 1785-1836 (SG)
        KILSBY UR (1662)
2121/1346   ZC 1795-1837; copies N
        KING'S CLIFFE (1821-1952) no trace
        KING'S SUTTON,Charlton see Charlton
        LONG BUCKBY UR (1707)
3190   ZC 1787-1837; ZC 1795-1836 (N)
        MAXEY - see under Peterborough
        MIDDLETON CHENEY (1844) now closed, no trace
        NASSINGTON (1839) viv 1946, now closed, no trace
        NORTHAMPTON,Doddridge UR (1662)
1142/1276/77   ZC 1770-1819,B 1820-37; ZC 1770-1829 (N)
        NORTHAMPTON,Abington Avenue UR (1777)
1275   ZC 1778-1837,B 1786-1836; copies N
        NORTHAMPTON,Commercial St (1829) united with Doddridge
1347   ZC 1830-37,B 1830-37;copies N   1959
        OLD (1720-1952)
904   ZC 1729-1837; ZC 1810-37 (N)
        ORLINGBURY (1830) now closed, no trace
        OUNDLE UR (1662) no pre-1850 registers
        PAULERSPURY (1826) viv 1946,no trace of records
        PETERBOROUGH,Westgate St UR (1776)
1278   ZC 1809-37; ZC 1810,1832-37 (N/H)
        PETERBOROUGH,Maxey Church UR (1809)   Apply Ch.Sec.
        POTTERSBURY & YARDLEY GOBION UR (1690)
2861/906   C 1739-1785,Z 1781-85,ZC 1785-1837,DB 1821-32
                Copies N

NORTHAMPTONSHIRE (Contd)

```
                ROTHWELL UR (1655)
2476/908              ZC 1776-1836,M 1692-1702 ; ZC 1811-37,M 1692-
                      1702 (N)
                SWINFORD (1810) now closed, no trace of records
                TOWCESTER UR (1794)
1783                  ZC 1794-1837; copies N
                WEEDON & FLORE UR (1662)
1281                  ZC 1787-1837; copies N
                WELDON CF nr Corby (1706)
2340                  ZC 1819-37; ZC 1824-37 (N)
                WELFORD,West End CF (1700)
1143/1282/3           C 1744-1792,ZC 1787-1837; C 1744-1837 (N)
                WELLINGBOROUGH,High St/Cheese Lane UR (1662)
911                   ZC 1783-1837,B 1792-1836; copies N
                WELLINGBOROUGH,  Salem  Chapel  (1812-72)  joined  with
                                              Cheese Lane in 1872
                WELLINGBOROUGH,West End (1789-1870)
2477                  ZC 1790-1837
                WILBARSTON - see Ashley
                WOLLASTON (1775-1923)
2047                  ZC 1788,1802-36 ; copies N
                YARDLEY GOBION - see under Potterspury
                YARDLEY  HASTINGS UR (1672)
2048                  ZC 1803-36; copies N
                YAXLEY UR (1822)                       Apply Ch.Sec.
                YELVERTOFT CF (1758)
2791                  ZC 1791-1837 + one burial; copies N
```

NORTHUMBERLAND

```
                     N = Newcastle Record Office
                     T = Tyne & Wear Record Office
RG4/
                ALNWICK,Zion Chapel (1731-1951)
                      C 1762-1837 (N)
                BERWICK-on-TWEED (viv 1850) no known records
                EMBLETON (viv 1850) no known records
                HAYDON BRIDGE UR (1816)
                      C 1817-1987 (N)
                HEXHAM,Ebenezer Chapel (1785-1966)
1578                  ZC 1787-1837; C 1787-1836 (N/SG)
                HORSLEY-on-TYNE UR (1662)
1580                  ZC 1785-1837; Z 1772-1800,C 1785-1837 (N)
                HOWDEN PANS Chapel 7 Willington Quays (1835) now closed
2484                  C 1835-37; copies N/T
                MORPETH,King St UR (1829)
                      ZC 1829-37; C 1829-72 (N) C 1829-37 (T)
                NEWCASTLE-on-TYNE,Postern Chapel now closed
1698/3453             ZC 1788-1837; C 1784-1837 (N/T)
                NEWCASTLE,St James' UR
3215                  ZC 1846-1836; C 1746-1872(T)
                NEWCASTLE,Zion Chapel (1820-29)
2681                  ZC 1821-29; copies N
                TYNEMOUTH,Bethel Chapel (1835-c58)
1404                  ZC 1835-37; C 1835-37 (N)
                TYNEMOUTH,St Andrew's Chapel (1817) now closed
2839                  ZC 1817-37
                WILLINGTON QUAY - see Howden Pans
```

NOTTINGHAMSHIRE

RG4/

    BAWTREY (1819) now closed
1410   ZC 1819-37; copies N
    GREASLEY,Moor Green & Kimberley UR (1662)
4447   ZC 1831-37; copies N
    HYSON GREEN (1824) now closed
47   C 1822-37,B 1824-37; copies N
    KEYWORTH,Christ Church UR (1768)
1582   ZC 1779-1837; copies N
    KIMBERLEY - see Greasley
    MANSFIELD WOODHOUSE (1802-58)
2487   ZC 1796-1836; ZC 1802-36 (N)
    MOOR GREEN - see Greasley
    NEWARK,Lombard St (1823-1932)
2865   ZC 1823-37
    NOTTINGHAM,Castle Gate CF (1687) now the Cong.Centre Ch
Various   C 1706-35,ZC 1734-1837,B 1831-37; C 1705-1959
                B 1790-1837 (N)
    NOTTINGHAM,Friar Lane Chapel (1827) now closed
1407   ZC 1804-37,B 1827-36
    NOTTINGHAM,Salem Chapel Barker Gate (1815) now closed
2844   ZC 1796-1837; copies N
    NOTTINGHAM,Sion Chapel Fletcher Gate (1796-1885)
138   ZC 1788-1834; copies N
    NOTTINGHAM,St James' St Chapel (1824 viv 1895) closed
2843   ZC 1823-37
    NOTTINGHAM,St Mary Gate Chapel now closed
1719/1590/1890 ZC 1772-1839
    RAMSKILL - see Bawtry
    RETFORD,EAST Chapel Gate (1808-1967)
3217   ZC 1813-36 ; C 1814-55 (N)
    SELSTON, Nottingham Rd UR (1670)
1591   ZC 1794-1837
    SUTTON-in-ASHFIELD UR (1651)
1592   ZC 1773-1837; copies N
    TUXFORD,Newcastle St (1840-59) no known records
    WORKSOP,Queen St UR (1831)
1412   C 1832-37; copies N

OXFORDSHIRE

RG4/

    ADDERBURY (1829-1956).No trace of records but linked
                                    with Banbury c.1885
    AMBROSDEN,Bethel Chapel IC (1825)   Apply Ch.Sec.
    APPLETON (1830) now closed. No trace of records
    BANBURY,Church Lane UR (1787)
2919/1593   C 1794-1806 ; copies O/L/SG
    BENSINGTON (1800-84)
3852   ZC 1835-36; copies O/B/L/SG
    BICESTER,Market End (1690-1957)
82   ZC 1786-1837,B 1786-1835; C 1695-1745,ZC 1785
                -1837,M 1695-96,B 1786-1835 ; O/B/L/SG/DWL
    BLACKTHORN (1825) now closed, no known records
    CHARLTON-on-OTMOOR (1827) closed, no known records
    CHINNOR EFCC (1805)
1594/2867/2920 ZC 1797-1837,B 1815 ; copies O/B/L/SG

```
                  DEDDINGTON IC (1842)                   Apply Ch.Sec.
                  FRILFORD UR (1841)                     Apply Ch.Sec.
                  GREAT BOURTON - see Wroxton
                  GREAT HAZELEY - see Wheatley
                  HENLEY - see Rotherfield Greys
                  LAUNTON IC (1807)                      Apply Ch.Sec.
                  MARSH GIBBON (1828) appeared closed by 1845.no trace
                  NETTLEBED (1834)          "        "         "
                  OXFORD,New Rd (1784) now Baptist
1784 & 1786            ZC 1784-1837,B 1785-1837; copies O/B/L/SG
                  OXFORD,George Lane (1830) now closed
2846                  ZC 1830-36; copies O/B/L/SG; C 1831-1932,
                      M 1837-1925,B 1837-98 (O)
                  OXFORD,Summertown (1813) Joined with George St 1897
                  PHEASANT'S HILL (1810-1871)  No trace of records
                  ROTHERFIELD GREYS   (1662)
1787/1710/1596        ZC 1719-1837,B 1685-1837; copies O/B/L/SG
                  ROTHERFIELD PEPPARD CF (1795)
                      C 1797-1877 (O/B/L/SG/DWL;
                  SKIRMITT (1824-75) combined with Pheasant's Hill.
                  STANFORD-in-the-VALE UR (1834)         Apply Ch.Sec.
                  STOKE ROW,Ipsden (1815) now closed
1597                  ZC 1818-33
                  TETSWORTH (1820-1968) no trace of records
                  THAME UR (1750)  No registers pre-1850
                  WATLINGTON merged with Tetsworth c.1899.no trace
                  WHEATLEY & GREAT HAZELEY UR (1841)     Apply Ch.Sec.
                  WITNEY Field House Chapel CF (1662)
                      ORCB 1806-21 (O); copies B/L/SG
                  WITNEY Independent & Baptist (1662)  now closed
2794/1602·            ZC 1799-1819,1823-36,D 1828 & 31; copies O
                  WROXTON & GREAT BOURTON now closed
1354/2894             ZC 1796-1837 ; copies O/B/L/SG
```

SHROPSHIRE

```
                  S = County Record Office Shrewsbury
                  W = Diocesan Records,St Helen's,Worcester
RG4/
                  AGDEN (1833-90) no trace of records
                  BISHOP'S CASTLE UR (1810)
2868                  ZC 1814-37; copies SG
                  BRIDGNORTH ,Stoneway Chapel UR (1662)
2921/2869             C 1769-1836,B 1822-37; copies S;
                      C 1769-1812 (SG)
                  BROSELEY (1837-1968) no known records
                  BROUGHALL ( 1819-1967) no trace of records
                  CHIRBURY,Marton Chapel CF (1829)
1606                  ZB 1829-36; C 1826-36 (SG)
                  CLIVE - see under Hadnall
                  CONDOVER - see under Dorrington
                  DORRINGTON,LYTHE HILL & CONDOVER (1806)
1525                  ZC 1808-37; copies S/W/SG
                  ELLESMERE,Victoria St UR (1786)
1609/1355             ZC 1788-1837; C 1787-1837(S); C 1787-1811(SG)
                  FRANKTON (1834) now closed
4467                  C 1835-37; copies SG
                  GABOWEN,Preshenlle Chapel UR (1831)
1536                  ZC 1832-36; C 1833-36 (SG)
                  GRIMPO (1831-70)
4467                  C 1833-36; copies SG
                  HADNALL & CLIVE (1821-1941)
4078                  ZC 1798-1837; copies S/W/SG
```

```
            HALES-OWEN now closed
1523                ZC 1805-37; copies S
            HODNETT & WOLLERTON UR (1800)
1539                ZC 1814-37; copies S
            LLANYBLODWEL,Smyrna Chapel (1825) now closed
4042                ZC 1825-36; copies S/W/SG
            LUDLOW,Corve St (1731-1967)
1524                ZC 1802-36,B 1826-36; C 1802-36 (S/W/SG
            LYTHE HILL - see Dorrington
            MAESBURY (1831) no trace of records
            MARKET DRAYTON now closed
1526                ZC 1776-1836; copies S/W
            MINSTERLEY CF (1795)
4043                ZC 1806-37; copies S/W/SG
            NANTMAWR (1830) now closed; no trace of records
            NEWPORT,Wellington Rd UR (1765)
3769                ZC 1828-37; copies SG
            OLDBURY appears closed by 1850
                    C 1715-1823 (S)
            OSWESTRY, Pant Chapel UR (1822)
2494                ZC 1829-36; copies S
            OSWESTRY,Old Chapel now Christchurch UR (1651)
1531/2870-1         ZC 1779-1837,B 1813-37; copies S
            OSWESTRY,Hermon Chapel WI (1837)          Apply Ch.Sec.
            PANT - see Oswestry
            PONTESBURY CF (1836)                      Apply Ch.Sec.
            PREES & WHIXALL UR (1800)
1537                ZC 1805-23; C 1805-37 (W/SG)
            PRESTON GOBALDS,Zions Hill Chapel now closed
141                 ZC 1827-36
            RUYTON-XI-TOWNS  UR (1833 - re-formed 1883)
                                                      Apply Ch.Sec.
            SHREWSBURY,Swan Hill Chapel CF (1662)
1706                ZC 1767-1837,B 1767-1854; C 1761-1837,B 1768-
                    1836 (S)
            SHREWSBURY, Bayston Hill UR (1834) no records pre-1850
            SHREWSBURY,Zion Chapel,Bomere Heath now closed
                    C 1827-37 (S)
            SHREWSBURY,Longden Chapel (1836) now closed, no trace
            WELLINGTON,Tanbank Chapel (1825) now closed
3609/2580           ZC 1829-37; copies S
            WEM, Chapel St UR (1775)
1534                C 1785-1837; copies S/W/SG
            WESTBURY - see under Minsterley
            WHITCHURCH, Doddington Chapel (1789) now closed
4044                ZC 1807-37; copies S
            WHITTINGTON -see Gabowen
            WHIXALL - see Prees
            WISTANSWICK UR (1805)                     Apply Ch.Sec.
            WOLLERTON - see Hodnett
```

SOMERSET
```
                    T = County Record Office Taunton

RG4/
            BARNTON St DAVIDS (1802-1958)      No trace
            BATH, Argyle St UR (1789)
Various         ZC 1785-1837,B 1800-38; copies T
            BATH,Combe Down IC (1815)              Apply Ch.Sec
```

```
                 BISHOPS HULL (1662-1922)
2054,1542/3          C 1733-1837,B 1774-1837; copies T
                 BISHOPS LYDIARD UR (1837)
                     C 1873+,M 1843+,B 1886+ (T)
                 BITTON,Oldland Common (1811)  now closed
3855                 ZC 1822-32
                 BRIDGWATER,Zion UR (1818)
1825                 ZC 1818-37,B 1823-37; copies T
                 BROADWAY (1739-1963)
1418                 ZC 1777-1840; copies T
                 BRUTON, Union Chapel (1803)  now closed
1545                 ZC 1802-37; copies T
                 CANNINGTON UR (1836)                  Apply Ch.Sec
                 CASTLE CARY,Zion Chapel (1816)  now closed, no trace
                 CHARD,High St Chapel (1700) now closed
1546/2690            ZC 1786-1837,  B 1812-18; C 1786-1982,B 1812-
                     1970 (T)
                 CHELWOOD (1721)  now closed
4079                 ZC 1721-1837; C 1721-1786 (T)
                 CLEVEDON, Hill Rd UR (1826)           Apply Ch.Sec
                 CLUTTON (viv 1850)  no trace of records
                 COMPTON DURDON (1841-1931)  no trace of records
                 DULVERTON CF (1662)
2056                 ZC 1831-36; copies T
                 FROME, Rook Lane & Trudox Hill CF (1662)
1730/1548            C 1793-1836, B 1831-36; C 1785-1837 (T)
                 FROME,Zion Chapel Whittox Lane UR (1773)
1549/3260            ZC 1786-1836; C 1793-1837,B 1801,1821 (T)
                 GALHAMPTON UR (1761)                  Apply Ch.Sec
                 GLASTONBURY UR (1662) Regs with Ch.Sec from 1840 only
                 ILCHESTER (1800-1961)
1553                 ZC 1807-37,B 1806-27;C 1807-1843,B 1806-41(T)
                 ILMINSTER,Providence Chapel (1812-37) reformed as Zion
2500                 ZC 1814-37; copies T
                 ILMINSTER,Zion Chapel (1837) closed c.1965
                     C 1837-1964,M 1837-1945,B 1859-1943 (T)
                 KINGSBURY EPISCOPI,Middle Lambrook Meeting UR(1680)
1556/2055/2057       ZC 1681-1697,1794-1837,M 1688-94 ;
                     C 1691-1837 (T);C 1681-1991,B 1744-1991(Ch)
                 KINGSDON (1665)  now closed
2349                 ZC 1809-34; copies T
                 KINGSTON St MARY (1821) now closed
3266                 ZC 1823-37,B 1828; copies T
                 LANGPORT UR (1833)
2501                 ZC 1832-37,B 1833-36; copies T
                 LONG ASHTON UR (1792)
1557                 ZC 1826-37; copies T

                 MARTOCK UR (1791)
1420                 ZC 1788-1837; copies T
                 MEARE IC (1826)                       Apply Ch.Sec
                 MIDDLE LAMBROOK UR - see Kingsbury Episcopi
                 MILBOURN PORT UR (1662)
1751                 ZC 1787-1837,B 1780-1837; C 1787-1837 (T)
                 MILVERTON (1784) now closed
2926                 ZC 1784-1837; C 1784-1837,B 1810+ (T)
                 NAILSEA UR (1839)                     Apply Ch.Sec
                 NORTH PETHERTON UR (1833)             Apply Ch.Sec
                 NORTON FITZWARREN UR (1835)
2873                 ZC 1826-37; copies T
                 NUNNEY,Trudox Hill CF(1670) - see also Frome
                     C 1760-1866,B 1800-1887 (T)
```

```
            OAKHILL (1837)  now closed
2876                ZC 1836-37; copies T
            OLDLAND COMMON - see Bitton
            PITMINSTER,Fulwood Chapel (1705-1964)
1421/2874           ZC 1709-48,1802-36; C 1705-93 (T)
            PORTISHEAD UR (1840)                    Apply Ch.Sec
            SHEPTON MALLET,Paul St Chapel (1830-1963)
2876                ZC 1830-35; C 1801-37,B 1802-1951 (T)
            SOMERTON,West ST UR (1734)
1562                ZC 1805-37,B 1807-37; copies T
            SOUTH CHERITON UR (1816)                Apply Ch.Sec
            SOUTH PETHERTON,Round Well St (1662)  now closed
2503,1563/4         ZC 1773-1837; C 1773-1860 (T)
            TAUNTON North St CF (1843)  no early records
            TAUNTON,Paul St UR (1662)
1567                ZC 1699-1837,B 1785-1837; C 1716-1837,M 1844-
                    59,B 1785-1837 (T)
            TEMPLECOMBE (1800)  now closed
3610                C 1816-36; copies T
            WELLINGTON,Lower Meeting UR (1730)
4046                ZC 1786-1837,B 1812-37; C 1786-1865,M 1847-78
                    B 1812-48 (T)
            WELLS Grove Lane UR (c 1785)
2122                ZC 1790-1836,B 1790-94; copies T
            WESTON SUPER MARE Boulevard UR (1827)
4047                ZC 1829-36; copies T
            WHITLEY BATCH (1721)  now closed
4079                ZC 1770-86
            WINCANTON (1725-1962)
2123/2352/2581      ZC 1798-1837,B 1815-25; copies T
            WINSCOMBE UR (1827)                     Apply Ch.Sec
            WINSHAM UR (1662)
2934                ZC 1810-37,B 1811-37; copies (T)
            WIVELISCOMBE EFCC (1662)
4048                ZC 1710-1837,B 1812-37; C 1709-68 (T)
            WRINGTON UR (1662)                      Apply Ch.Sec
            YEOVIL,Princes St UR (1662)
1793                ZC 1794-1836; C 1794-1911,B 1843-60 (T)
```

STAFFORDSHIRE

```
                 S = County Record Office,Stafford
            NB There are no Congregational records held at
                    either Lichfield or Walsall
RG4/
            ABBOTTS BROMLEY (1830)
                    C 1825-1977,B 1839-1956(S)
            ALTON,Providence Chapel (1809-70)
2877                ZC 1811-37; copies S
            ARMITAGE (1817)  now closed
3291                C 1821-27; copies S
            AUDLEY,Halmerend (1817)  no trace of records
            BILSTON Oxford St now Portway Rd CF (1760)
3198                ZC 1785-1837; copies S
            BRANSTON  UR (1834)                     Apply Ch.Sec
            BREWOOD (1805-40)
2932                ZC 1810-37; copies S
            BROWNHILLS UR (1816)                    Apply Ch.Sec
            BURSLEM,Salem Chapel (1821) now Moorland  Rd UR
2717                ZC 1823-37; ZC 1826-31 (Hanley Library)
            BURTON-on-TRENT,High St now Trinity UR (1662)
3439                ZC 1808-37; copies S
```

```
              CANNOCK UR (1817)
2879              ZC 1816-37; copies S
              CHEADLE,Bethel CF (1797)
2880              C 1800-37; copies S
              CHECKLEY,Ebenezer, Deadman's Green (1821-30)
4070              ZC 1822-30; copies S
              ECCLESHALL (1800)  now closed
4049              ZC 1822-36; copies S
              GREAT BARR, Allen Memorial UR (1808)    Apply Ch.Sec
              GORNAL,Sedgeley UR (1778)
2354              ZC 1778-1837;ZC 1815-37,B 1792-1837(S)
              HANDSWORTH,Union Church (1788)  now closed
1869/70           ZC 1788-1837,B 1827-37; copies S
              HANLEY,Tabernacle  (1784) comb with Presbyterians 1900,
                                                    now closed
1871/2881         ZC 1786-1837; copies Hanley Library
              LEEK,Derby St (1695) UM from 1977
1872              ZC 1785-1837,DB 1797-1837; copies S
              LEEK,Union St (1833)  now closed
2353              C 1830-37; copies S
              LICHFIELD,Wade St UR (1808)
1738/3297         ZC 1801-37; copies S
              LICHFIELD,Whittington Chapel (1840) merged with Wade St
              LONGTON,Caroline  St (1818) merged with Trentham Rd  UR
                                                                  1964
                  ZC 1819-37( Hanley Library)
              NEWCASTLE-u-LYME,The Marsh Chapel CF (1781)
1873              ZC 1777-1836; copies Newcastle Library
              OVER TEAN,Providence UR (1822) now UM  from 1986
3304              ZC 1803-37; copies S
              RUGELEY,Providence Chapel (1820)  now closed
2859              ZC 1821-37; copies S
              RUGELEY,St Paul's UR (1794) UM from 1976  Apply Ch.Sec
              SHELTON - see Stoke-on-Trent
              STAFFORD,Zion Chapel, now Eastgate UR (1786)
3616/3089         ZC 1795-1828,C 1829-37; copies S
              STOKE-on-TRENT, Caroline Chapel  now closed
3613              ZC 1819-37
              STOKE-on-TRENT,Hope Chapel,Shelton (1812)  now closed
2723              ZC 1809-37; copies Hanley Library
              STOKE-on-TRENT, Tomkin Chapel UR,Bagnall (1837)
                                                    Apply Ch.Sec
              STONE,Chapel St UR (1786)
1874              ZC 1787-1837; CM 1787-1837 (S)
              TAMWORTH,Aldergate St (1826)  later Unitarian
1427(under Warwick) ZC 1827-1836; copies S
              TEAN - see Over Tean
              TUTBURY,Back St Chapel CF (1777)
2727              ZC 1801-37; copies S
              UTTOXETER,Carter St UR, formerly Bear Lane (1788)
2928              ZC 1793-1836
              WALSALL,Bridge St Chapel (1763-1945)
2702              ZC 1785-1837; copies S
              WEDNESBURY,Trinity Chapel (1750) now closed,no trace
              WEST BROMWICH,Ebenezer (1700) joined with Mares Green
                                                              1971
1875              C 1787-1837; C 1803-36, B 1835-6 (S/SG)
              WEST BROMWICH,Mares Green (1664) now Hardware St UR
1700              ZC 1786-1837,B 1837; ZC 1787-1837 (S/SG)
              WHEATON ASTON (1806)  now closed, no trace of records
```

```
                WOLVERHAMPTON,Queen St Chapel (1809-70)
1428                ZC 1785-1836; copies S
                WOLVERHAMPTON,Temple St, now Penn UR (1782)
1740                ZC 1771-1836,B 1786-99; copies S
                    CM 1849-64, Wolverhampton Library
                WOLVERHAMPTON,Wall Heath UR(1841)      Apply Ch.Sec
                WORDSLEY - see Stourbridge,Worcs
```

SUFFOLK

```
                    B = Bury St Edmunds Record Office
                    I = Ipswich Record Office
RG4/
                ALDERTON (1836-1948)    no known records
                ALDHAM (1767-1948)      no known records
                ASHFIELD (1671) now closed, no known records
                BARROW (1836 viv 1850) now closed,no known records
                BECCLES UR (1652)
1832/2961           ZC 1703-1837; copies B/I
                BELSTEAD (1790 viv 1850) no known records
                BERGHOLT,EAST CF (1689)
3618/1895           C 1689-1836,B 1825-36; copies B/I
                BOXFORD UR (1824)
3619                ZCB 1824-37; copies B/I
                BRAMFIELD UR (1841)               Apply Ch.Sec.
                BRANDESTON (1828-1967)
3617                ZC 1819-37; copies B/I
                BUNGAY UR (1658)
1834/1894/3037      C 1796-1850,B 1786-1850; copies B/I
                BURY St EDMUNDS,Northgate & Whiting St Chapels (now UR)
Various             ZC 1785-1837,B 1808-37;  copies I;  ZC 1656-
                    1928,B 1650-1721 (B);
                CLARE,Old Meeting UR (1687)
1837/1866/2137      ZC 1799-1837,B 1785-87,1811-37; copies B/I
                COMBS UR (1780)
                    C 1871-80 (I)
                COWLINGE (1836) now closed, no trace
                CRATFIELD (1812-56)
2128                ZC 1813-37; copies B/I
                DEBENHAM UR (1662)
3093                ZC 1706-1837,B 1821-31; copies B/I
                DENHAM (1671) closed by 1850, no known records
                DUNWICH (1671) closed by 1850, no known records
                EAST BERGHOLT - see Bergholt,East
                EDWARDSTONE - see Boxford
                ELMHAM,SOUTH (1653) closed by 1850, no known records
                EYE (1671) closed by 1850, no known records
                FALKENHAM (1836 viv 1850) now closed, no trace
                FINBOROUGH (1810) Re-formed 1862,now UR  Apply Ch.Sec
                FOXEARTH (1836-1952) no trace of records
                FRAMLINGHAM,Old Meeting UR (1717)
1838/9 & 3620       ZC 1710-14,1745-1837,B 1702-1836; copies B/I
                FRESSINGFIELD (1651) closed by 1850, no trace
                GISLINGHAM (1671) closed by 1850, no trace
                GLEMSFORD (1726-1952) no trace of records
                GORLESTON (1818 viv 1911) now closed
1896                ZC 1828-36,B 1830-37; copies B/I
                HADLEIGH UR (1688)
3621/3704/3926      C 1690-1837; copies B/I
                HALESWORTH UR (1793)
1342                ZC 1796-1837; copies B/I
                HAUGHLEY UR (1835)
                    C 1842-1903 (I)
```

SUFFOLK (Contd)

```
          HAVERHILL,Old Chapel UR (1662)
1843/4,1794/1845    C 1709-83,ZC 1783-1839,B 1790-1814
          HAVERHILL,West End CF (1836)
1843                ZC 1834-37; copies B/I
          HINTLESHAM (1767-1923) no trace of records
          IPSWICH,St  ,New Chapel CF (1793) merged with  Hatfield
                                                          Rd (1903)
2583                ZC 1828-37,B 1820-37
          IPSWICH,Christ Church,Tackett St (1686) now closed
1848/9,1795         ZC 1708-1837,B 1759-1858; copies B/I
          KESSINGLAND (1671- closed by 1850) no known records
          KNODISHALL (1671- closed by 1850) no known records
          LAVENHAM (1697) now closed
1852                ZC 1735-1835,B 1827-35; copies I/SG;
                    C 1739-1960,B 1827-81 (B)
          LOWESTOFT,Old Meeting UR (1665)
3624                C 1726-33,ZC 1813-36; copies B/I/SG
          MELFORD,LONG UR (1662)
1852-4/2883         ZC 1733-1837,B 17685-1822; copies B/I/SG
          NACTON (1829-1968) no trace of records
          NAYLAND (1690) now closed
1355                ZC 1785-1836; copies B/I
          NEEDHAM MARKET UR (1662)
4452                ZC 1833-37; copies B/I
          NEWMARKET (1787) now closed
2963                ZC 1787-1837; copies B/I
          OULTON BROAD (1837-1968) no known records
          PEASONHILL (1671) closed by 1850, no known records
          RATTLEDEN (1671) no known records
          RENDHAM (1650-1952) merged with Badingham
Various             C 1723-1838,B 1765-1803; copies B/I
          RACKINGHALL (1671) closed by 1850, no records
          SHELLEY (1767-1956) no known records
          SIBTON (1671) now closed, no records known
          SOUTHWOLD UR (1695)
1860/2358/3096      ZC 1730-1837; copies B/I
          STANSFIELD (1835) now closed
2357                ZC 1834-37; copies B/I; ZC 1834+,B 1835+ (B)
          STOWMARKET,Ipswich St UR (1719)
2707/8             ZC 1780-1838; copies B/I
          STOW UPLAND UR (1810)_                    Apply Ch.Sec.
          SUDBURY,Old Meeting,Friar St CF (1662)
1861/3623/4081      ZC 1707-1837; copies B; C 1707-1957,M 1838-53
                    B 1739-1858 (B)
          SWEFFLING (1671) no known records
          WALPOLE (1646 viv 1850)
Variouis            ZC 1706-99,1806-37; copies B/I
          WATTISFIELD UR (1654)
1863/4              ZC 1735-1837; ZC 1678-1893,B 1678-1893 (B)
          WHATFIELD (1767) no known records
          WICKHAM MARKET (1814) now closed
2964                ZC 1820-37; copies B/I
```

WICKHAMBROOK UR (1682)
1865   C 1726-1837; copies B/I; B 1821-64 (B)

WINSTON (1671) now closed, no known records
WISSETT (1841) closed, no known records
WOODBRIDGE,Beaumont Chapel (1793-1899)
1866   ZC 1794-1837,B 1793-1837
WOODBRIDGE,Quay Meeting UR (1651)
2584   ZC 1710-1837,B 1779-1837; copies B/I
WRENTHAM UR (1649)
1867/3098   ZC 1650-1837; copies B/I; ZC 1650-1700 (SG)

SURREY

                    GL = Guildhall Library
                    GLR = Greater London Record Office
                    GM = Guildford Muniment Office
                    K = Surrey County Record Office Kingston
RG4/

BLETCHINGLEY (1826-1946) no trace of records
CHARLWOOD UR (1814)
1898   C 1817-37,B 1832-35; copies GLR/GM/SG
CHERTSEY,Windsor St UR (1662)
1899   Z 1775-1837,C 1758-1837,B 1783-1837 ;
              copies GM/K/SG
CROYDON,Salem,George St UR (1689)
2204/3301   C 1797-1836,B 1832; copies GLR/GM/K/SG
DORKING,West End UR (1662)
3102/3626/7   Z 1736-1843,C 1718-1843,M 1729-1801,B 1730-
              1855 ; copies GLR/GM/SG
ELSTEAD UR (1834)
2205   ZC 1834-37; copies GLR/GM/SG
EPSOM,Church St UR (1688)
2206   Z 1819-36,C 1826-37,B 1829-36; copies GLR/SG
EPSOM,Little Chapel (1779-1811)
2362/2715/2363/44   ZC 1779-1811,B 1807; copies GLR/GM/SG
EWHURST (1821-1958)
2209   ZC 1823-36
FARNHAM,Ebenezer UR (1792)
1701   ZC 1794-1837,DB 1827-36; ZC 1794-1837 (GM/SG)
FARNHAM,Filday Chapel (1821-1963) no known records
GODALMING,Harts Lane later Bridge Rd UR (1690)
3103   ZC 1786-1836,B 1786-1828; copies GM/SG
GOMSHALL & SHERE UR (1821)
2209   ZC 1823-37; ZC 1823-40 (GM/SG)
GUILDFORD,Blackhorse Lane,now Chapel St UR (1672)
3427   C 1707-33,M 1770-73,B 1708-72; copies GM/SG
GUILDFORD,New Chapel,North St (1802) now closed
2207   Z 1801-37,C 1803-38; copies GM/SG
HASLEMERE UR (1792)
2060/2210   ZC 1789-1834; C 1789-1836,D 1808-24 (GM/SG)
KINGSTON-upon-THAMES UR (1662)
12/1744/1746 Z 1785-1802,C 1690-1803; copies GM/SG;
              C 1698-1803 (GL)
KINGSTON-upon-THAMES,Heather St Chapel(1687) now closed
2061/2125/2211/3104 Z 1776-1836,C 1776-1857,B 1802-36,1839-55;
              C 1776-1857,B 1802-55 (GL)

```
              LEATHERHEAD,Christ Church UR (1829)
2212              ZC 1827-37,B 1832-37; copies GL/GM/SG
              MERTON,Salem Chapel - see London South
              MITCHAM,Zion Chapel,Western Rd now closed
                  B 1821-94 (GLR)
              MITCHAM,London Road (1815-1940)
                  C 1819-93,B 1821+ (GLR)
              MORTLAKE,Vernon Rd UR (1672)
3628              C 1719-52 ; copies GL/GM/SG
              OXTED,Paine Hill Chapel  now closed
2213/4            ZC 1824-36

              REIGATE,High St,now Reigate Park UR (1662)
1900              ZC 1835-37; copies GL/GM/SG
              RICHMOND,The Vineyard CF (1830)
2890              Z 1812-36,C 1831-36; Z 1812-36 (GM/SG);
                  C 1831-36 (GL)
              SHAMLEY GREEN (1824) no known records
              SHERE - see Gomshall & Shere
              SUTTON,Trinity UR (1799) no known records before 1878
              THAMES DITTON (1804) closed by 1947
4128              C 1816-36; Z 1787-1836,C 1816-36 (GL/GM/SG);
                  C 1837-64 (K)
              WESTCOTT,nr Dorking (1840-1961)  no known records
              WOKING (1778-1836)  no known records
              WORPLESDON,Normandy Chapel (1822) now closed
2217              C 1823-37; copies GL/GM/SG
```

SUSSEX

```
                  E = East Sussex Record Office
                  W = West Sussex Record Office
RG4/
              ALFRISTON,Ebenezer Chapel UR (1801)
2218              C 1801-37,B 1804-36; ZC 1801-37,B 1804-68 (E)
                  Z 1799-1815,C 1815-37 (SG)
              ARDINGLEY CF (1822)
2587              C 1816-37
              ARUNDEL,Tarrant St Chapel (1780) now closed
1879              C 1796-1837; copies SG
              BATTLE (1842-80) joined with Burwash in 1880
                  no trace of early records
              BILLINGSHURST UR (1815)
2365/2939         ZC 1813-27,B 1821-36
              BOGNOR REGIS,Hanover Chapel UR (1813)
2885              C 1827-36; copies SG
              BOREHAMSTREET (1811-1850) no trace
              BOSHAM UR (1837)
2124              C 1823-36; C 1823-83 (W/SG)
              BRIGHTON, Hanover Chapel (1825) now closed
3105/3134/5       C 1826-38,B 1825-54; copies SG
              BRIGHTON, Hove Chapel (1824)  now closed,no trace
              BRIGHTON, Tabernacle West (1834) now closed, no trace
              BRIGHTON,Union Chapel Ship St (1662)
3423/3106/3272    C 1700-1837, B 1803-37;C 1700-1858,M 1837-53,
                  B 1800-22 (E); C 1700-1811 (SG)
              BRIGHTON,Zion Chapel (1826) no trace
              BRIGHTON,Zoar Chapel (1841) no trace
                  NOTE:The  present BRIGHTHELM UR church is  an
amalgamation of at least three of the above chapels;apply Ch.Sec.
```

	BURGESS HILL,St John's Common (1829) no trace
	BURWASH Independent Calvinist Chapel (1713) joined with
2219	ZC 1767-1835; copies E/SG Battle
	BUXTED (1800) now closed, no trace of records
	CHICHESTER,Ebenezer Chapel now closed
	C 1849-70,M 1839-57 (W)
	CHICHESTER,West Lane UR (1771)
2220	C 1783-1836; C 1783-93,1881-1916 (W)
	CHIDDINGLY (1820-84)
2364	C 1835
	COPTHORNE(1828-1964) no trace, but replaced by Countess of Huntingdon Chapel
	CUCKFIELD,Providence Chapel (1832) now closed
3630	C 1825-37; C 1821-37 (SG)
	EAST GRINSTEAD,Zion Chapel (1811-1964) no trace, but check with Moat Church UR
	HARTING (1800-1935)
2887	C 1827-37; copies SG
	HASTINGS,Croft Chapel (1805-1954)
1424/1429	C 1818-54,B 1817-55; C 1818-54(E/SG); MIs 1816+ (W)
	HEATHFIELD (1767) closed by 1909
3107	C 1775-1837,B 1824-37; copies E
	HELLINGLY Independent Calvinist (1828 - closed by 1845)
39/2364	ZC 1830-37,C 1835; copies E/SG
	HENFIELD (1832-1965)
1902	C 1832-37; copies SG
	HERSTMONCEUX (1811) now closed
3111	ZC 1812-37,B 1829-31; C 1812-37,1859-(E) C 1812-37 (SG)
	HORSHAM UR (1776)
Various	C 1776-1800,1812-37,B 1827-36; C 1776-1800, 1817-37 (SG)
	LEWES,Tabernacle UR (1817)
2850	C 1817-37,B 1820-36; C 1817+ (E)
	LEWES, Cliffe Chapel closed 1859
2063	C 1812-14; ZC 1819-38 (E)
	LINDFIELD (1814-58) linked with Ardingly
2587	C 1816-37
	NEWHAVEN (1797-1958) no trace of records
	PARTRIDGE GREEN closed by 1845
1902	C 1832-37
	PETWORTH (1740 viv 1855)
3364	C 1827-37; Z 1785-1837,C 1827-37 (SG)
	RINGMER UR (1835) Apply Ch,Sec.
	ROGATE (1826 - closed by 1846) no trace
	RYE,Watch Bell St Chapel (1817 viv 1845)
2983	ZC 1819-37; C 1819-38 E/W/SG
	SEAFORD UR (1823) Apply Ch.Sec.
	SLINFOLD,Hayes Chapel closed by 1845
2365	ZC 1813-27; copies SG
	TURNERS HILL (1824-1965) no trace
	WATERSFIELD,Nr Pulborough (1823) closed, no trace
	WISBOROUGH GREEN closed by 1953
2624	C 1822-35; copies SG
	WIVELSFIELD,Oak Hall Chapel (1779-1965)
3145/1709	C 1789-1831,ZC 1832-35; C 1789-1831 (W)
	WORTHING,Chapel St now Shelley Rd UR (1804)
3200	ZC 1808-37

WARWICKSHIRE

W = County Record Office,Warwick
B = Birmingham Reference Library
S = Shakespeare Birthplace Trust Stratford

RG4/

ANSLEY UR (1824)   see also Hartshill
ZC 1824-37,C 1841-1912 (W)
ATHERSTONE UR (1794)
3201   ZC 1796,B 1827-36;ZC 1796-1900,B 1794-1925(W)
ATTLEBOROUGH (1722) now closed, no known records
BADDESLEY ENSOR UR (1801)
3632   ZC 1801-36; copies W
BEDWORTH,Old Meeting UR (1686)
2971/2944   ZC 1688-1837,B 1826-37; copies W;ZB 1810-1960
BIRMINGHAM, Carrs lane UR (1748)   (W)
2891   C 1806-37;C 1785-1862,B 1831-59 (B)
BIRMINGHAM, Elmwood UR (1803)   Apply Ch.Sec.
BIRMINGHAM,Erdington (1814) Now UR in Holly Rd
4106/3639   C 1822-36,1838-56;C 1822-36,1857-1975 (B);
C 1822-56 (W)
BIRMINGHAM, Ebenezer,Steel House Lane (1803-1932)
2892   ZC 1817-37; C 1828-1931 (B)
BIRMINGHAM, Lozells Chapel,Wheeler St (1840-viv 1864)
No known records
BISHOP'S ITCHINGTON CF (1834)
C 1842+,Z 1843+ with church secretary
BRINKLOW UR (1827)
C 1843-1909 (W)
BULKINGTON EFCC (1811)
2949   ZC 1811-36; copies W
CHURCHOVER (1822-1951)
2625   ZC 1822-36; copies W
COLESHILL UR/UM (1835)
3638   C 1833-37; copies W
COVENTRY,Vicar Lane now Warwick Rd UR (1662)
2980   ZC 1757-1837; copies W
COVENTRY,West Orchard Chapel UR (1776)
3314   ZC 1766-1836,B 1799-1837; copies W
COVENTRY,Foleshill Rd UR (1795)
3316   ZC 1793-1837; ZC 1788-1837 (W)
COVENTRY,Well St (1827) Joined with Vine St 1946
No known records
COVENTRY,Potters Green UR (1816)   Apply Ch.Sec.
HAMPTON-in-ARDEN UR (1825) no regs before 1893
HARTSHILL,Chapel End UR (1807) Linked with Ansley
3317   ZC 1789-1837; copies W; C 1841-1912 (W)
HOCKLEY HEATH (1837-79)   no known records
KENILWORTH,Abbey Hill UR (1720)
2805   C 1831-36; copies W
KINETON now closed; Members List 1813-93 (W)
LEAMINGTON SPA,Spencer St UR (1816)
2952   ZC 1830-37;C 1828-37,B 1836-71 (W)
LEAMINGTON,Mill St (1829-86) joined with Spencer St
No early records

	LONG COMPTON,Ebenezer Chapel CF (1820)
2976	ZC 1820-36; C 1820-63,B 1846-55 (W)

LONG COMPTON,Ebenezer Chapel CF (1820)
2976   ZC 1820-36; C 1820-63,B 1846-55 (W)
LONG ITCHINGTON CF (1828)
               C 1832-1966 (W)
LOXLEY (1816-32) no trace of records
MINSHULL now closed
               C 1809-24 (W)
NUNEATON,Zion Chapel Coton Rd (1817)
2977   ZC 1818-36; copies W
NUNEATON,Bond St Chapel (1817-1901) no trace
POLESWORTH, High St Chapel CF (1832)
2894   ZC 1832-36; copies W
RADFORD SEMELE UR (1825)   Apply Ch.Sec.
SHEEPY MAGNA (1816-1922) no trace of records
SHOTTERY (1833) now closed, no trace
SOLIHULL,Bethesda Chapel (1825) later Christchurch UR
2893   ZC 1836-37; copies W
SOUTHAM CF (1832)
               C 1844-53,Members registers 1840+ with church
STOKE,Harefield Rd UR (1813) no early records
STRATFORD-on-AVON UR (1662)
1713   ZCB 1786-1836; copies W/S; C 1864-80 (S)
STRETTON-under-FOSSE (1662-1968)
2589/2954/5   ZC 1787-94,1797-1836,B 1788-1790;
               CMB 1787-1836 (W)
WARWICK,Brook St (1758) later Unitarian
3640/1   ZC 1784-1837,B 1806-37; C 1784-1889,B 1806-84
                                                          (W)
WILMCOTE (1802) now closed. No trace of records
WILNEYCOTE (1816) now closed, no trace of records
WITHYBROOK (1840-1951) no trace of records

WESTMORLAND - see under CUMBERLAND

WILTSHIRE
               T = County Record Office Trowbridge
RG4/
ATWORTH (1789 - closed by 1893)
2221   ZC 1790-1836; copies T
AVEBURY (1670) now closed
3642   ZC 1807-37; copies T
BEARFIELD CF (1787) , orig. Countess of Huntingdon's
3429   C 1791-1837,B 1837-56
BRADFORD-on-AVON,Morgan's Hill UR (1740) UM 1977
2222/3/4   ZC 1772-1837;Copies T; D 1772-92,B 1830-33(T)
BRINKWORTH (1742-1951) no known records
BROADCHALKE UR (1808)
2225   ZC 1808-36; copies T
BULFORD EFCC (1805)
2957   ZC 1806-37; copies T
CASTLE COMBE CF (1743)
4420   ZC 1785-1836; copies T
CHAPMANSLADE,Lower Meeting (1761) now closed
2226   C 1765-1837,B 1826-37; ZC 1785-1837,B 1787-
               1837 (T)
CHIPPENHAM, Tabernacle UR Emery lane (1770)
2227   C 1791-1837,B 1826-37; ZC 1790-1837 (T)

	CHRISTIAN MALFORD (1767) later linked with Malmesbury
2130	ZC 1809-36; copies T
	CODFORD St MARY (1778-1964)
2228	ZC 1813-36; copies T
	COLERNE (1824-1968)
2229	ZC 1801-37; copies T
	CORSHAM,St Aldelm's UR (1690)
	No early records
	CORSHAM,Monks Chapel UR (1662)
2897	ZC 1787-1836,B 1793-1836
	CORSTON (1821-1947) no trace of records
	CRICKLADE UR (1799) UM 1969,no records before 1878,
	DEVIZES,St Mary's UR (1772)
2591/3328	ZC 1774-1837,B 1796-1805,1819-37;
	C 1774-1833,D 1774-1833,B 1819-37 (T)
	DONHEAD St MARY closed by 1850
1904	ZC 1800-37; copies T
	DURRINGTON EFCC (1820) Apply Ch.Sec.
	EAST KNOYLE (1840-49) no known records
	EBBESBOURNE WAKE IC (1783)
2368	ZC 1783-1837; copies T
	FORD (1820-1968) no known records
	FOVANT UR (1820)
2369	ZC 1816-36; copies T
	HAWKRIDGE CF (1840) Apply Ch.Sec.
	HEYTESBURY (1812-1964)
2592	ZC 1811-37; C 1811-37 (T)
	HIGHWORTH,Zion Chapel UR (1777)
2593	ZC 1820-36; copies T
	HINDON (1810-1971) no known records
	HOLT,The Street UR,(1810)(Nr Bradford) Apply Ch.Sec.
	HORNINGHAM CF (1566)
1905	ZC 1784-1837,B 1787-1836; copies T
	HULLAVINGTON (1821) now closed
2233	ZC 1825-36; copies T
	LAYCOCK,St Stephens UR (1783) Apply Ch.Sec.
	LITTLETON DREW closed by 1850
2234	ZC 1825-37
	LYNEHAM,Clack Chapel(1777) closed by 1850
2236	ZC 1810-36; copies T
	MAIDEN BRADLEY,Church St UR (1780)
2594	ZC 1825-37; copies T
	MALMESBURY,St Mary's St UR (1662)
2595	ZC 1812-37; copies T
	MARKET LAVINGTON Trinity UR (1805) UM 1984
3330	ZC 1797-1836; copies T
	MARLBOROUGH,New Rd UR (1817) UM 1984
3329	ZC 1824-37; copies T
	MELKSHAM,High St UR (1773) UM 1975
3331	ZC 1778-1837; copies T
	MERE,Boar St Chapel UR (1795)
2240	ZC 1796-1837; copies T
	SALISBURY,Fisherton St UR (1662)
1717/2014	ZC 1757-1837,B 1786-1803; copies T
	SALISBURY,Endless St now closed
1906/2898	ZC 1807-37; copies T
	SHERSTON,Cliff Rd Chapel CF (1825) Apply Ch.Sec.
	SUTTON VENEY (1793-1969)
2596	ZC 1801-37; C 1801-37 (T)

	SWINDON, Immanuel UR Newport St (1804)
2243	ZC 1803-37,B 1812-34; copies T
	TISBURY,High St UR (1726) UM 1978
4108	ZC 1723-1837; ZC 1721-53,1765-1837 (T)
	TROWBRIDGE,Tabernacle UR (1767) UM 1968
3318	ZC 1773-1837,B 1785-1837; copies T
	WARMINSTER,George St UR (1719) UM 1984
3276	ZC 1772-1837; copies T
	WESTBURY,Warminster Rd UR formerly Old Meeting(1719)
2742/3277	ZCB 1779-1837; ZC 1779-1837,B 1785-1837 (T)
	WESTBURY,Upper Meeting (1762-1840)
2741/3513	ZC 1769-1837,B 1769-1804; ZC 1769-1837,
	B 1769-1833 (T)
	WILTON,St Edith's UR (1700) UM 1966
2988	ZC 1753-1836,B 1815-36; C 1753-1836,
	B 1815,1825-36 (T)
	WOOTON BASSETT UR (1825)
3278	ZC 1826-36; C 1826-35 (T)

YORKSHIRE, EAST

B = Beverley Record Office
D = Doncaster Record Office

RG4/

	BEVERLEY,Lairgate UR (1700)
2601/3515/3668	C 1701-80,ZC 1780-1837; C 1701-1868 (B)
	BRIDLINGTON,Zion Chapel CF (1662)
3020/3333	C 1698-1836,M 1708-16,B 1698-1716,1776-1818
	1826-30
	COTTINGHAM, Zion UR (1690)
Various	C 1690-1706,1713-20,1734-85,1792-1837
	COWICK,Ebenezer Chapel (1838-93)
	ZC 1830-33,B 1837 (B)
	DRIFFIELD,Providence CF (1801)
2998	ZC 1801-37; copies B
	ELLOUGHTON UR (1810)
	ZC 1801-29 (B)
	GOOLE,Zion UR (1828)
3163	ZC 1829-37; copies B
	HORNSEA,Bethesda UR (1807)
3066	ZC 1820-37; copies B
	HOWDEN,Providence Chapel (1662) now closed
2148	ZC 1781-1836,B 1797-1833; copies B
	HULL,Ebenezer Chapel Dagger Lane (1662) - Presbyterian
	after 1783 ; closed 1817
	ZC 1668-1782,1789-1817,B 1798 (B)
	HULL,Fish St UR (1769)
3388	ZC 1769-1837
	HULL,Holborn St Chapel (1830) now closed
3225/RG8.102A	ZC 1809,C 1830-47,M 1838-51,B 1830-52;
	HULL,Providence Chapel Hope St (1763) - moved 1903, now
	closed
Various	ZC 1769,1789-1837,B 1799-1837; copies B
	HULL,Salem Chapel Cogan St (1832-1913)
1914/RG8.102B	ZC1833-37,DB 1833-5,; ZC 1828-1901,M 1837-83,
	B 1833-47 (B)
	HULL,Trinity Chapel Nile St (1813-34)
3648	ZC 1813-29,B 1821-34; copies B
	MARKET WEIGHTON (1809-1956)
1723	ZC 1819-37; copies B
	NORTH FRODINGHAM (1814) now closed
2660	ZC 1826-36,B 1816-35; copies B

RILLINGTON (1818-1962)
1921   ZC 1819-37
SCULCOATES,Tabernacle (1827) now closed
4107   ZC 1826-34,B 1827-36; DB 1827-37 (B)
SKIPSEA (1801-1969)
2012   ZC 1807-36; copies B
SOUTH CAVE UR (1662)
2765   ZC 1784-1831; C 1791-1836 (B)
SWANLAND UR (1693)
2769   ZC 1739-1836; copies B
THORNE (1800-1931)
              C 1805-1931 (D)

YORK,Lendal Chapel formerly Jubbergate,(1798)now New
                                        Lendal UR(1934)
4055/4451   ZC 1798-1837,B 1828-36

YORKSHIRE, NORTH

                   C = Cleveland Record Office
                   N = Northallerton Record Office
                   W = Wakefield Record Office
RG4/

ALDBOROUGH,Nr Boroughbridge   closed by 1860
2603   C 1802-37; C 1843-57 (W)
APPLETON WISK viv 1850 no trace of records
AYTON,GREAT,Cleveland viv 1850 now closed
3147   ZC 1763-1836
BROTHERTON (1833) now closed
3437   ZC 1833-37
DACRE - see Pateley Bridge
DENT UR (1810) now in Cumbria
2638   ZC 1808-36
EASINGWOLD (1814-78)
3079   C 1820-36
EGTON Nr Whitby, viv 1850 no trace of records
GRASSINGTON CF (1811)
3007   ZC 1811-37
GREEN HAMMERTON,Nr Knaresboro' (1797-1955)
2604   ZC 1798-1836,B 1801-36
GUISBOROUGH,Bethel Chapel (1798) ; now Westgate UR
3647   ZC 1799-1834; copies C
HAWES (1843) viv 1850 no trace of records
HARROGATE,Prospect Place Chapel (1817) now closed
2074   ZC 1817-35,B 1824
KELD-in-SWALEDALE UR (1815)
3232   ZC 1790-1836
KIRBY MOORSIDE,Tinley Garth Chapel (1812-1951)
2144   ZC 1814-37
KNARESBORO',Windsor Lane Chapel (1779) now closed
3398   ZC 1780-1836
KNOTTINGLEY,Nr Ferrybridge (1807) now closed
3649   ZC 1813-37
LAZENBY (1835-77) no trace of records
LEYBURN (1795-1960)
3650   ZC 1810-36
LOFTHOUSE (1827) West Road UR
3652   ZC 1832-37

```
                MALTON,Ebenezer Chapel (1815-1967)
3074                    ZC 1814-37
                MICKLEBY (1811) nr Whitby  now closed
2647                    ZC 1814-36
                MIDDLESBOROUGH viv 1850 now Linthorpe UR; apply Ch.Sec
                NEWTON (1696) nr Pickering  now closed
2659                    ZC 1791-1837
                NORTHALLERTON,Zion Chapel UR (1806)
2607                    ZC 1805-37; C 1806-47,B 1836-52 (N)
                PATELEY BRIDGE,Providence UR,Dacre (1816)
3679                    ZC 1813-37
                PICKERING,Hungate UR (1788)
3714                    C 1789-1837
                REETH nr Richmond (1784-1964)
2750                    ZC 1787-1837

                RIMSWICK,Zoar Chapel Hindswell (1829)  now closed
2608                    ZC 1830
                RIPON,All Hallowgate (1818-1915)
1923                    ZC 1818-37
                RIPON,Providence Chapel (1813)
3682                    Z 1821-36,D 1828-36
                ROBIN HOOD'S BAY UR (1840)              Apply Ch.Sec
                SCARBOROUGH,Old Meeting (1703-1925)
3660/2754              ZC 1703-1837,M 1705-20
                SEDBERGH,Salem Chapel (1825)  now in Cumbria ; closed
2755                    ZC 1825-37
                SETTLE (1816)  now closed
3741                    ZC 1816-37,B 1821-36
                SKIPTON,Zion UR (1770)
3743/2087/3696     C 1783-1837,ZC 1792-1857,DB 1837-56
                SOWERBY,Old Chapel (1839-1957)  no trace of records
                STAITHES,Bethel Chapel (1823)  now closed
2610                    ZC 1827-37; copies C
                STOCKTON-on-TEES, Green Dragon Yard  now closed
                       ZC 1799-1816,B 1820-36 (C)
                STOKESLEY & GUISBOROUGH - see Guisborough
                SUTTON,Ebenezer Chapel,Thirsk (1808-77)
2611                    ZC 1808-31
                SWALEDALE,Low Row Chapel (1693) formerly Swarsbed Hall
3211                    ZC 1766-1837,B 1822-35
                THIRSK (1805-1962)
2200                    ZC 1805-37
                WHITBY,Silver St (1770) now Westcliff CF/UR
2820                    ZC 1770-1837
                WINTERBURN (1704)  now closed
2616                    ZC 1811-36
```

YORKSHIRE, SOUTH

```
                        D = Doncaster Record Office
                        S = Sheffield Record Office
RG4/
                ATTERCLIFFE,Zion Chapel (1800-1969)
4435                    ZC 1794,1798-1837; C 1798-1837 (S)
                BARNSLEY,Ebenezer Chapel (1778-1962)
3667                    ZC 1783-1830,B 1785-1837; copies S
                BARNSLEY,Salem Chapel (1824)  now closed
3285                    ZC 1818-37,B 1834-37; copies S
                CLAYTON,High Hoyland Chapel UR (1790)
3148/9                  ZC 1797-1837,DB 1797-1835
```

2639	DONCASTER,Ebenezer Chapel UR,Hallgate (1798) ZC 1798-1837; C 1798-1884 (D)
2373	DONCASTER,Providence Chapel (1813) now closed C 1812-34; C 1814-34 (S)
	FULWOOD - see Sheffield
	GREASEBOROUGH - see Rotherham
2073	HANDSWORTH,Woodhouse Chapel (1820) now closed ZC 1823-37; copies S ; CMB 1852+ (S)
	LOXLEY - see Sheffield
	MASBOROUGH - see Rotherham
3656	OUGHTIBRIDGE UR (1833) ZC 1833-40,B 1838-40; C 1833-40 (S)
	ROTHERHAM,Independent Chapel (1777) now closed C 1816-37 (S)
	ROTHERHAM,Greasborough UR (1815) Apply Ch.Sec
3236/7	ROTHERHAM,Masborough UR (1758) ZC 1758-1837,B 1763-1794;C 1758-1822, B 1763-94 (S)
3179	SHEFFIELD, Fulwood Chapel (1729-1877) ZC 1820-37; C 1827-37,B 1793,95 (S)
2761	SHEFFIELD,Garden St Chapel (1803) now closed C 1804-37; C 1804-36 (S)
2757	SHEFFIELD,Howard St Chapel (1789-1903) ZC 1780-1839,B 1795-1838; copies S
2083/4	SHEFFIELD,Lee Croft Chapel (1797-1862) ZC 1785-1837,B 1789; C 1785-1818,B 1789,1828, 1836 (S)
	SHEFFIELD,Loxley Chapel UR(1793) C 1831-1985,B 1830-1985 (S)
2758	SHEFFIELD,Mount Zion Chapel now closed ZC 1818-37; C 1835-37,M 1869-77 (S)
Various	SHEFFIELD,Nether Chapel (1714-1963) C 1748-89,ZC 1790-1837,B 1786-1816;C 1748- 1837,M 1869-1944,B 1800-16,1869-1971 (S)
3690	SHEFFIELD,Queen St Chapel (1783) now closed ZC 1783-1837; C 1783-1956 (S)
4110/2768	STANNINGTON,Underbank Chapel later Unitarian now closed ZC 1718-1837,C 1718-77; C 1718-77 (S)
3209	STOCKBRIDGE,Ebenezer Chapel (1819) now closed C 1829-37; copies S
2771	THORNE,Ebenezer Chapel (1800-1968) C 1805-37; copies S
2772/3	THURLSTONE,Netherfield Chapel now closed C 1788-1825,ZC 1824-37,B 1809-19,1830-36; C 1788-1954,M 1840-92,B 1803-10,1830-1954 (S)
	WEST MELTON (1796) now closed C 1795-1837 (S)
	WOODHOUSE - see Handsworth

YORKSHIRE, WEST

L = Leeds Record Office
S = Sheffield Record Office
W = Wakefield Record Office

RG4/	
56	ADDINGHAM (1829) now closed Z 1829-36
3857	ALLERTON,Nr Bradford (1814) ZC 1815-37

```
              BATLEY, Hanover St UR (1839)
                       C 1840-43 (W)
              BINGLEY, Dryden St UR (1695)
3383                   B 1754-1837
              BIRSTALL, Community Smithies Lane CF(1832)Apply Ch.Sec
              BOSTON SPA (1837-1946)  no known records
              BRADFORD, Eccleshill UR (1823)
3001                   ZC 1824-34,B 1823-37; C 1823-56,B 1823+ (W)
              BRADFORD,Horton Lane Chapel (1787-1954)
3139                   CB 1783-1833,Z 1820-31,CB 1833-37; C 1783-
                       1951,B 1783-1853 (W)
              BRADFORD,Zion Chapel UR Wibsey (1841)
                       C 1843-1984,B 1840-1973 (W)
              BRADFORD,,Wyke UR Westfield (1826)
                       C 1846-1912,M 1848-1973,B 1843-86 (W)
              BRIGHOUSE,Bramley Lane  now closed
                       C 1831-37 (W)
              BRIGHOUSE,Bridge End  (1778) now closed
3146                   ZC 1782-1837,B 1788,1800-37
              BURLEY-in-WHARFEDALE,Salem UR (1839)
                       CMB 1858+ (W)
              CLECKHEATON,Birstall UR (1710)
2636/3034         C 1724-1837,B 1783,1803-37
              COWICK,Ebenezer Chapel,Snaith (1838-93)
2072                   ZC 1830-33
              ECCLESHILL - see Bradford
              ELLAND,Providence Chapel UR (1822)      Apply Ch.Sec
              FLOCTON,Zion Chapel UR (1802)
3161                   ZC 1795-1836
              FULWOOD - see Sheffield
              GISBURN,Sandy Skye Chapel (1812)  now closed
3063                   C 1812-37,B 1814-37
              GOMERSAL,The Grove UR (1825)
3064                   ZC 1827-37
              HALIFAX,Booth Chapel (1761)  now closed
3169                   ZC 1785-1837,B 1785-93
              HALIFAX,Mount Zion Chapel Bramley Lane(1823) now closed
3349                   ZC 1831-37
              HALIFAX,Zion Chapel Wade St (1816-1959)
2605                   ZC 1797-1837 ; C 1818-1959,B 1817-1922 (W)
              HALIFAX,Square Chapel (1760-1969)
3168/1703         ZC 1763-1837,B 1771-1837

              HECKMONDWIKE,Old Chapel UR (1674)
3173                   ZC 1786-1837,B 1781-90
                       C 1787-1957,B 1797-1801 (W)
              HOLMFIRTH,Lane Chapel UR (1770) Upperthong
3032                   ZC 1779-1837; C 1779-1916 (W)
              HONLEY,Cotton Chapel UR (1795)
3387                   ZC 1795-1837
              HOPTON - see Mirfield
              HORTON -in - CRAVEN CF (1689)
2743                   ZC 1773-1837,B 1794-1832
              HUDDERSFIELD,Ramsden St UR (1772)
3137                   ZC 1824-38; C 1824-1932 (W)
              HUDDERSFIELD,Clayton West - see Clayton
              IDLE,Upper Chapel (1690)  now closed
2643              C 1783-1837
              IDLE,Upper Chapel Calverley (1790)  now closed
3391                   C 1797-1837
```

```
          KEIGHLEY (1730-1964)
3394/5          ZC 1749-1837
          KIRKBURTON,Dogley Lane Chapel (1816)   now closed
3670            ZC 1816-37
          KIRKBURTON,Upper Church (1795)   now closed
3396/7          C 1795-1837,B 1798-1820,1823-37
          LEEDS,Bethel Chapel (1802) now closed
2646            ZC 1802-37; C 1802-37 (W)
          LEEDS,Bethel Chapel Wortley   now closed
1916            ZC 1796-1838; C 1802-55,B 1802-55 (L/W)
          LEEDS,Call Lane now West Park UR (1672)
3674/3723       C 1672-1835)
          LEEDS,Campfield Chapel (1824-1936) no known records
          LEEDS,George St Chapel   now closed
3673            ZC 1807-37; C 1807-37 (W/SG)
          LEEDS,Queen St formerly Whitehall Chapel,now closed
3399/3676       ZC 1756-1837
          LEEDS,Salem Chapel Hunslet Lane (1784)   now closed
4064            ZC 1825-37
          LIGHTCLIFFE, Leeds Rd UR (1830)          Apply Ch.Sec
          LIVERSEDGE,Lower Chapel (1789)   now closed
3402            ZC 1786-1837,B 1797-1814
          MARSDEN,Buckley Hill UR (1790)
403             ZC 1796-1837; C 1796-1948 (W)
          MARTIN TOP (1816)   now closed, no known records
          MIRFIELD,Hopton UR (1731)
2650            ZC 1733-1837,B 1785-94
          MIXENDEN, Moor End UR Nr Halifax (1688)
3405/2193       ZC 1742-1837,B 1768-1837; C 1742-1837,B 1829-
                                                    37 (W)
          MORLEY,Reheboth (New Chapel)   closed   1971
3734A/2652/3482   Z 1775-1886,ZC 1785-1806,1811-37,B 1785-1810;
                  C 1785-1967,B 1834-1971 (W)
          MORLEY, Old Chapel (1650)   now closed
Various         C 1654-1760,ZC 1745-1837, B 1676,1755-83 ;
                C 1656-1960,B 1656-1957 (W); C 1654-1830,
                                    B 1654-1888 (DWL)
          NORTHOWRAM,Heywood (1672)   now closed
Various         ZC 1744-71,1774-1837,B 1822-37; C 1744-1837
                                                    (W)
          OSSETT,The Green (1717)   now closed
2745/3076       ZCB 1749-88,ZC 1765-1837,B 1817-34
          OTLEY,Bridge St UR (1821)
3738            ZC 1822-37
          OVENDEN,Providence UR (1837)
1920            ZC 1837; C 1837 (W)
          PONTEFRACT,Ebenezer Chapel (1662)   now closed
3739            ZC 1819-37,B 1812-37
          PUDSEY,New Chapel (1792)   now closed
3077            ZC 1831-37
          RASTRICK,Bridge End Chapel (1800)   now closed
                C 1782-1837,1890-1975,B 1800-37,1848-1971 (W)
          SADDLEWORTH,Providence Chapel (1806)   now closed
2082/3414       ZC 1806-37
          SADDLEWORTH,Ebenezer Chapel (1831) now closed
2817            C 1832-37
          Saddleworth,formerly in the West Riding,now in Lancs
          SHELLEY UR Nr Huddersfield (1790)
                C 1759-1851,B 1798-1846 (S)
          SOWERBY,Old Sowerby Chapel (1645) now closed
                C 1740-1977 (W)
```

SOYLAND,Blackshaw Chapel   now closed
                C 1819-37
              STAINLAND (1755)   now closed
2767   ZC 1779-1836,B 1783-1837; C 1779-1871,B 1786-
                                                      1836 (W)
              STANSFIELD,Eastwood Chapel (1699)   now closed
                C 1771-1837,B 1779-1837 (W)
              THORNTON,Bradford Kipping (1664)   now closed
Various   C 1756-1834,ZC 1807-37,B 1756-1803,1819-33
                CMB 1867+ (W)
              WAKEFIELD,New or Zion Chapel UR (1782)
2777/8   ZC 1782-1837,B 1783-1837; C 1782-1941,M 1838
                                        -99,B 1783-1931 (W)
              WAKEFIELD,Quebec Chapel   now closed
1926   C 1830-34
              WAKEFIELD,Salem Chapel   now closed
3705/4052   ZC 1799-1836
              WARLEY Nr Halifax   now Highroadwell UR
2019   ZC 1748-1837,B 1756-1837; C 1760-1937,M 1862-
                                      1936,B 1751-1979 (L/W)
              WILSDEN Nr Bradford,Low Chapel   now closed
3936   ZC 1793-1837,B 1816-37; C 1793-1847,B 1793-
                                                      1947 (L)

WALES

```
                NLW = National Library of Wales,Aberystwyth
ANGLESEY
           NB No Independent Chapel records are at present held
              at the Anglesey Record Office Llangefni
RG4/
                AMLWCH,Carmel WI (1785)
1683                     ZC 1790-1837
                AMLWCH, Saron WI (1842)                 Apply Ch.Sec
                BEAUMARIS, Seion WI (1785)
3548/3784               ZC 1791-1837
                BODEDERN,Saron WI (1812)                Apply Ch.Sec
                BODFFORDD,Sardis WI (1810)              Apply Ch.Sec
                BODORGAN,Capel Mawr WI (1763)           Apply Ch.Sec
                BRYNGWRAN, Salem WI (1790)              Apply Ch.Sec
                BRYNSIENCYN,Libanus WI (1840)           Apply Ch.Sec
                CEFN-COCH,Seilo WI (1837)               Apply Ch.Sec
                CEMAIS,Bethel WI (1806)                 Apply Ch.Sec
                GAERWEN,Berea WI (1839)                 Apply Ch.Sec
                GWALCHMAI,Moreia WI (1844)              Apply Ch.Sec
                HOLYHEAD,Tabernacle WI (1817)
4088                    ZC 1809-37
                HOLYHEAD,Tabor (1847)  now closed, no trace of records
                LLANDDANIEL,Cana WI (1821)
3783                    ZC 1825-36
                LLANDDEUSANT,Bethania WI (1790)         Apply Ch.Sec
                LLANNERCH-Y-MEDD,Peniel WI (1775)
2901                    ZC 1803-37
                LLANFACHRETH,Bethesda WI (1832)         Apply Ch.Sec
                LLANFAIR, Neubwll WI (1840)             Apply Ch.Sec
                LLANFAIR P.G.,Ebenezer WI (1839)        Apply Ch.Sec
                LLANFECHELL,Ebenezer WI (1778)          Apply Ch.Sec
                LLANFAELOG,Rehoboth WI (1835)           Apply Ch.Sec
                LLANGADWALADR,Hermon WI (1813)
3783                    ZC 1818-37
                LLANGEFNI,Ebenezer WI (1744)
2902                    ZC 1798-1837,B 1798
                LLANGRISTIOLUS,Paradrys  now closed
4003                    ZC 1785-91,1829-37,B 1836
                LLECHYLCHED,Salem now closed
3788                    ZC 1799-1837
                MAENADDWYN,Hebron WI (1827)             Apply Ch.Sec
                MAES-Y-LLAN,Bethel (1845)  now closed
                MOELFRE,Carmel WI (1822)                Apply Ch.Sec
                PENMYNEDD,Horeb WI (1819)               Apply Ch.Sec
                PENTRAETH,Ebenezer WI (1800)
3545                    ZC 1823-37
                RHOS-FAWR,Soar WI (1815)                Apply Ch.Sec
                RHOS-GOCH,Seion (1837)  now closed
                RHOS-MEIRCH - see Llangefni
                TALWRN,Siloam WI (1839)                 Apply Ch.Sec
```

BRECON

Area Record Office is Llandrindod Wells, but at present
no original or PRO copies for Brecon chapels are being held there

```
RG4/        ABERGWESYN,Moreia WI (1829)              Apply Ch.Sec
            ABERYSGIR (1838)   now closed, no trace
            BAILIHALOG (1700)   now closed, no trace
            BETHANIA UR (1841)                       Apply Ch.Sec
            BEULAH WI (1842)                         Apply Ch.Sec
            BRECHFA UR (Llandyfalle Parish) (1791)   Apply Ch.Sec
            BRECON, Plough Chapel UR/WI (1699)
3798                ZC 1795-1837,D 1820-22
            BRECON,Libanus UR (1823)
2250                ZC 1827-37
            BRYCHGOED,Senni WI (1740)
3543                ZC 1775-1837; copies SG
            BUILTH, Horeb UR (1808)
3799                ZC 1805-37
            CEFN-Y-BEDD UR (1835)                    Apply Ch.Sec
            CERRIG-CADARN UR (1812)
3939                ZC 1824-37
            CWMCAMLAIS Sardis WI (1840)              Apply Ch.Sec
            CWM-RHOS (1808)   now closed, no trace
            CWM-WYSG Saron WI (1824)                 Apply Ch.Sec
            DYFFRYN CROWNON,Llangynidr(1842)   now closed,no trace
            HAY-on-WYE Ebenezer UR (1846)            Apply Ch.Sec
            LLANAFAN FAWR,Troedrhiwdalar WI (1689)
                    Ch.Register of Members 1781-1848 (NLW)
            LLANELLI,Siloam WI (1828)
4441                ZC 1829-37
            LLANGATWG,Carmel WI (1768)
3940                ZC 1826-37
            LLANGYNIDR - see Dyffryn Crownon
            LLANVIGAN   now closed
3800                ZC 1792-1837
            LLANWRTYD,Penuel WI (1832)
2343                ZC 1834-37
            LLYWEL,Saron   now closed
1725                ZC 1815-37,B 1833-37
            MAESMYNYDD,Salem UR (1825)               Apply Ch.Sec
            MAES-YR-ONNEN UR (1640)                  Apply Ch.Sec
            MERTHYR CYNOG Ebenezer UR (1805)
3052                ZC 1802-37
            OLEWYDD WI (1847)                        Apply Ch.Sec
            PENNORTH UR (1841)                       Apply Ch.Sec
            TALGARTH,Bethania UR (1811)
3802                ZC 1814-37
            TALGARTH,Tredwstan WI (1687)
3801                ZC 1700-1837,B 1708-1837
            TAL-Y-BONT,Bethel   now closed, no trace
            TAF-FECHAN (1829)   now closed, no trace
            TYN-Y-COED WI (1770)                     Apply Ch.Sec
            TRECASTLE,Soar WI (1850)                 Apply Ch.Sec
            TRETOWER (1844)   now closed, no trace
            TROEDRHIWDALAR - see Llanafan Fawr
```

BRECON (Contd)
```
            VAYNOR,Bethlehem  now closed
2251              ZC 1827-37
            YR ABER (Llanfigan parish) (1762)   now closed, no trace
            YSTRADFELLTE,Hermon WI (1798)            Apply Ch.Sec
```

CAERNARFONSHIRE
```
            C = Caernarfon Record Office
            D = Dolgellau Record Office
RG4/
            ABER-ERCH Ebenezer WI (1822)          Apply Ch.Sec
            ABER-SOCH WI (1831)                   Apply Ch.Sec
            BANGOR,Bethel  now closed, no trace
            BANGOR, Beulah WI (1836)              Apply Ch.Sec
            BANGOR,Ebenezer IC (1790)
3832/2518        ZC 1790-1837; copies C
            BETHESDA,Bethania WI (1820)           Apply Ch.Sec
            BETWS-Y-COED,Nantybeniog WI (1837)    Apply Ch.Sec
            BONTNEWYDD,Libanus WI (1821)          Apply Ch.Sec
            BRWYNOG,Siloh (1824)   now closed, no trace
            BWLCHTOCYN WI (1796)                  Apply Ch.Sec
            CAERNARFON,Pendref WI (1726)
2254/4116        ZC 1785-1837;  C 1785-1903  (C);copies  D
            CAPEL NEWYDD WI (1772)
3537/3484/5      ZC 1791-1837,B 1831-37; copies C
            CARMEL, Pisgah WI (1820)              Apply Ch.Sec
            CEIDIO, Peniel WI (1823)              Apply Ch.Sec
            CHWILOG,Siloh WI (1835)               Apply Ch.Sec
            CLYNNOG,Nasareth WI (1823)
3834             ZC 1834-37; copies C
            CONWY,Seion (1835)  now closed, no trace
            DEINIOLEN,BETHEL WI (1810)
3838             ZC 1815-37; copies C
            DEINIOLEN, Ebenezer(WI) (1823)
3839/40          ZC 1822-37; copies C

            DOLWYDDELLAN,Bethel WI (1826)
3836             ZC 1817-36; copies C
            DRWYS-Y-COED,Nantlle WI (1836)            Apply Ch.Sec

            DWYGYFYLCHI,Horeb WI (1820)
4468             ZC 1804-37; copies C
            FELINHELI,Siloh (1834)  now closed, no trace
            GLAN CONWY,Peniel WI (1833)           Apply Ch.Sec
            GLASINFRYN,Bethmaaca WI (1836)        Apply Ch.Sec
            GROESLON ,Gosen WI (1849)             Apply Ch.Sec
            HENRYD WI (1823)                      Apply Ch.Sec
            LLANBEDR,Salem WI (1806)              Apply Ch.Sec
            LLANBEDROG,Seion WI(1849)             Apply Ch.Sec
            LLANBEDRYCENNIN,Salem WI (1806)       Apply Ch.Sec
            LLANBERIS,Jerwsalem (1829) WI
3442             ZC 1832-37; copies C
            LLANDEGAI,Amana WI (1845)             Apply Ch.Sec
            LLANDEINIOLEN - see Deiniolen
```

CAERNARFONSHIRE (Contd)
```
          LLANENGAN WI - see also Pwllheli
3538          ZC 1815-37; copies C
          LLANGELYNIN,Henryd & Seion WI (1823/35)
4089          ZC 1819-36,D 1836; copies C
          LLANGWNADI,Hebron WI (1821)              Apply Ch.Sec
          LLANGYBI,Capel Helyg WI (1652)
3841          ZC 1829-37; copies C
          LLANGYBI,Sardis (1822) joined with Capel Helyg
          LLANIESTYN,Rehoboth WI (1807)            Apply Ch.Sec
          LLANLLECHID,Bethesda    now closed
4027          ZC 1790-1837; copies C
          LLANLLECHID,Carmel WI (1839)             Apply Ch.Sec
          LLANLLYFNI,Nasareth WI (1823)            Apply Ch.Sec
          LLAN-RUG, Bryngwyn WI (1830)             Apply Ch.Sec
          LLANRWST,Nebo WI (1833)                  Apply Ch.Sec
          LLANRWST,Siloam WI (1800)                Apply Ch.Sec
          LLANRWST,Tabernacle WI (1800)            Apply Ch.Sec
          LLANSANFFRAID, Peniel WI (1833)          Apply Ch.Sec
          LLANWNDA,Saron WI (1801)                 Apply Ch.Sec
          LLANYSTUMDWY,Rhoslan WI (1808)
4422/3842     ZC 1813-37; copies C
          LLANYSTUMDWY,Tabernacle IC (1831)        Apply Ch.Sec
          MOELTRYFAN,Hermon WI (1840)              Apply Ch.Sec
          MORFA BYCHAN,Siloam WI (1829)            Apply Ch.Sec
          MYNYDD LANDEGAI, Amana WI (1845)         Apply Ch.Sec
          NANT-Y-RHIW WI (1800)                    Apply Ch.Sec
          NEFYN,Soar WI (1823)
3843          ZC 1823-37; copies C
          OLD COLWYN,Ebenezer WI (1814)
4026/3835     ZC 1805-37,B 1817-37; copies  C
          PENCAENEWYDD,Sardis-closed but see LLangybi
          PENMORFA,Seion WI (1840)                 Apply Ch.Sec
          PENHRYN DEUDRAETH,Carmel (1840) closed, no trace
          PENTIR,Peniel WI (1831)                  Apply Ch.Sec
          PENTREFELIN,Tabor (1826)  now closed
          PENTREFOELAS,Bethel WI (1804)            Apply Ch.Sec
          PEN-Y-GROES,Soar WI (1834)               Apply Ch.Sec
          PORTHMADOG,Salem WI (1827)
4028          ZC 1826-37; copies C
          PWLLHELI,Pen-lan (1650)
3537/3485/6   ZC 1791-1837,B 1831-37; copies C
          RHIW,Nebo WI (1813)                      Apply Ch.Sec
          RHOS-LAN - see Llanystumdwy
          TAL-Y-BONT, Bethlehem WI (1785)          Apply Ch.Sec
          TAL-Y-SARN,Saron WI (1822)               Apply Ch.Sec
          TREFOR, Maesyneuadd WI (1810)            Apply Ch.Sec
          TREFRIW,Ebenezer WI (1790)               Apply Ch.Sec
          TUDWEILOG,Beersheba (1825)  now closed
          WAUNFAWR,Moriah WI (1829)
2783          ZC 1828-37; copies C
```

CARDIGANSHIRE

A = Aberystwyth Record Office

```
RG4/
            ABERAERON,Peniel WI (1833)              Apply Ch.Sec
            ABERYSTWYTH, Penmaenglas (1818-78) replaced by
                      Seion WI in 1878 - see below
            ABERYSTWYTH,Bryn Mair WI (1833)         Apply Ch.Sec
            ABERYSTWYTH,Seion WI,Baker St
3420              ZC 1804-37; copies A
            BOW STREET WI (1815)                    Apply Ch.Sec
            BRON-Y-GWYN,Trewen closed 1816 - see Troedyraur
3803              C 1785-1816; copies SG
            BRYNGWENITH WI (1834)                   Apply Ch.Sec
            BRYNGWYN,Betws parish WI (1841)         Apply Ch.Sec
            BRYN MORIAH WI (1848)                   Apply Ch.Sec
            BRYNRHIWGALED WI (1781)                 Apply Ch.Sec
            BRYN-TEG, Llanybydder parish WI (1833)  Apply Ch.Sec
            BWLCH-Y-GROES WI (1833)                 Apply Ch.Sec
            CAPEL-Y-WIG WI (1813)                   Apply Ch.Sec
            CARDIGAN,Capel Mair WI (1803)           Apply Ch.Sec
4008              ZC 1803-37; copies A
            CARDIGAN,English Congregational (1837) - closed
            CELLAN WI (1811)                        Apply Ch.Sec
            CILCENNIN,Seion WI (1775)               Apply Ch.Sec
            COED GRUFFYDD,Salem WI (1824)
3420              C 1834 only
            CWM-ANN,Bethel (1839)  now closed, no trace
            CYDBLWY, Penrhiwgaled  now closed
3805              ZC 1818-37; copies A
            DIHEWYD, Bethlehem WI (1840)            Apply Ch.Sec
            DRE-FACH, Bethel WI (1810)              Apply Ch.Sec
            DYFFRYNPAITH,Beulah (1832) - see Llanbadarn Fawr
            FELIN FACH, Ty'n-y-gwndwn WI (1773)
4012              ZC 1821-37; copies A
            FELIN FACH, Troed-y-rhiw WI (1808)      Apply Ch.Sec
            GLYNARTHEN WI (1797)
                  C 1836-1930 (NLW)
            LAMPETER, Soar WI (1841)                Apply Ch.Sec
            LLANBADARN FAWR,Zoar & Clarach (1802)
3420/4010         C 1813-16,ZC 1815-37; copies A
                  C 1850-1971 (NLW)
            LLANBADARN FAWR,Beulah (1832)
                  C 1815-50 (NLW)
            LLANDYSUL,Carmel WI                     Apply Ch.Sec
            LLANDYSUL,Horeb WI (1784)
1684              C 1797-1837,ZC 1819-37; copies A
            LLANFAIRCLYDOGAU,Capel Mair WI (1825)   Apply Ch.Sec
            LLANGYBI,Ebenezer WI (1772)
4011              ZC 1821-37; copies A

            LLANGWRYFON (1843)  now closed, no trace
            LLAN-NON,Nebo WI (1808)                 Apply Ch.Sec
            LLANARTH,Pen-y-Cae WI (1826)
                  C 1841-1974,B 1839-69 (NLW)
```

             LLANDYGWYDD,Bethel (1840) now closed, no trace
             LLECHRYD, Old Chapel WI (1709)   Apply Ch.Sec
             MAEN-Y-GROES WI (1828)   Apply Ch.Sec
             MYDROILYN WI (1753)   Apply Ch.Sec
             NEUADD-LWYD WI (1746)
3808/9   C 1791-1837; copies A/SG ; C 1791-1896 (NLW)
             PANTYCRUGIAU WI (1848)   Apply Ch.Sec
             TALGARREG,Pisgah WI (1821)   Apply Ch.Sec
             TAL-Y-BONT,Bethel WI (1805)
4663/3420   ZC 1805-37; copies A; C 1805-63 (NLW)
             TAL-Y-BONT,Seion (1835) closed, no trace
             TRE-Y-WEN,Ceredigion Brngwyn
                   C 1819-1880,B 1848-1889 (Carmarthen RO)
             TROEDYRAUR (1808) - see also Bron-y-Gwyn
3053   ZC 1814-37; copies SG
             TY'N-y-GWNDWN - see Felin Fach
             Y DRE-WEN WI (1737)   Apply Ch.Sec

         ZC 1828-37

# CARMARTHENSHIRE
         C = Carmarthen Record Office

RG4/
             ABERGORLECH WI   Apply Ch.Sec
             ABERGWILI,Ebenezer WI (1833) inc.Pantleg & Peniel
3815   ZC 1814-37; Copies C; C 1886-1957 (C)
             ABERNANT, Bwlch-Newydd WI (1746)
4123   ZC 1805-41; Copies C
             AMMANFORD Christian Temple WI (1782) Apply Ch.Sec
             BLAEN-y-COED WI (1807)   Apply Ch.Sec
             BRECHFA,Horeb WI (1829)   Apply Ch.Sec
             BRONGWYN,Trewen now closed
                   C 1819-80,B 1848-89 (C)
             BRYN SEION WI (1831)   Apply Ch.Sec
             CAPEL NONNI WI (1810)   Apply Ch.Sec
             CARMARTHEN,Hoet Awst WI, Lammas St (1688)
1685/6   C 1792-1837; C 1792-1907,B 1792-5 (C)
             CARMARTHEN,Peniel WI (1809)   Apply Ch.Sec
             CARMARTHEN,Philadelphia WI (1809)   Apply Ch.Sec
             CARMARTHEN,Union St WI (1847)   Apply Ch.Sec
             CEFNARTHEN WI (1689)   Apply Ch.Sec
             CRUG-Y-BAR WI (1763)   Apply Ch.Sec
             CRWBIN,Ebenezer WI (1829)   Apply Ch.Sec
             CYNGHORDY,Bethel WI (1813)   Apply Ch.Sec
             CYNWIL,Hermon WI (1744)   Apply Ch.Sec
             DRE-FACH,Capel Seion WI (1712)   Apply Ch.Sec
             EFAIL-WEN,Nebo WI (1836)   Apply Ch.Sec
             ESGAIRDAWE (1755) now closed joined with
             FFALD-y-BRENIN WI (1792)
                   C 1818-57,B 1838-44 (C)
             FFYNNON-BEDR WI (c1808)   Apply Ch.Sec
             GWERNOGLE,LLanfihangel WI (1749)
                   C 1813-21 (NLW)

```
              GWYNFE,Jerwsalem WI (c1695)
4016                ZC 1822-37 ; copies C
              GWYNFE,Bethlehem WI (1773)              Apply Ch.Sec
              HENLLAN AMGOED WI (1697)
2516/3771         C 1748-1837,B 1785-1829; Copies C
              HENDY-GWYN,Tabernacle WI (1849)         Apply Ch.Sec
              KIDWELLY,Capel Sul WI (1785)
                  C 1788-1918,B 1838-1916 (C)
              LAUGHARNE,Philadelphia (1809)(English)
4015              ZC 1825-37; ZC 1820-37 (C)
              LLANGYNNWR,Rama WI (1839)               Apply Ch.Sec
              LLANBOIDY WI(1800) linked with Henllan Amgoed
              LLANDEILO,Capel Isaac (1689)  now closed
3774/3823         ZC 1779-1837; copies C
              LLANDEILO,Hermon WI (1813)
4017/18           ZC 1806-37,D 1814,34; ZC 1828-37 (C)
              LLANDEILO,Salem WI (1817)               Apply Ch.Sec
              LLANDEILO,Tabernacle WI (1817)          Apply Ch.Sec
              LLANDOVERY,Salem WI (1797)
3822              ZC 1804-37 ; copies C
              LLANDDOWROR,Elim WI (1832)              Apply Ch.Sec
              LLANEDI,New House (1712)  now closed
3819              ZC 1734-1837,B 1776,1785-95 ; CB 1745-1837(C)
              LLANEGWAD,Horeb (1830)  now closed
              LLANELLI,Bryn WI (1841)                 Apply Ch.Sec
              LLANELLI,Capel Als WI (1780)
1687/4060         ZC 1808-37,DB 1831-37; C 1837-1904,M 1837-70
                  B 1842-51 (NLW/C)
              LLANELLI,Park UR (1839)(English)        Apply Ch.Sec
              LLANELLI,Siloa WI (1841)
                  C 1890-1909,(C)
              LLANFAIR-ar-y-BRYN  now closed
3824              ZC 1769-1837,DB 1833 ;C 1731-1837,B 1731-55(C)
              LLANFIHANGEL,Ararth & Pencader WI
2257              ZC 1825-37; copies C
              LLANGADOG,Bethleham WI (1800)           Apply Ch.Sec
              LLANGADOG,Providence WI (1840)          Apply Ch.Sec
              LLANGELER,Saron WI (1756)
                  C 1802-34,1850 (NLW)
              LLANGELER,Seilo WI (1825)               Apply Ch.Sec
              LLANGENNECH,Bethesda WI (1831)          Apply Ch.Sec
              LLANGLYDWEN,Hebron & Pen-y-Groes  now closed
3773              ZC 1818-37,D 1819-31; CMB 1850-85 (NLW)
              LLANGWYNNWR (1809)
                  C 1819-65 (NLW)
              LLANGYNOG,Bethesda (1773)  now closed, no trace
              LLAN-NON,Bethania WI (1800)
                  C 1800-37 (C); C 1800-1926 (NLW)
              LLAN-NON,Llwyn-Teg WI (1845)            Apply Ch.Sec
              LLANPUMPSAINT,Nebo WI (1841)            Apply Ch.Sec
              LLANSADWRN,Carmel WI (1830)             Apply Ch.Sec
              LLANSADWRN,Ebenezer WI (1830)           Apply Ch.Sec
```

1688	LLANSTEPHAN,New Chapel WI formerly Bethel ZC 1814-37; copies
	LLANWINIO,Moriah (1830) now closed, no trace
4020	LLANWRDA,Tabor WI(1792) ZC 1800-37
3826/4021	LLAN-Y-BIDDAR,Rhyd-y-Bont WI (c1715) C 1775-1825,ZC 1818-37; copies C
	LLAN-Y-BRI, Capel Newydd WI (1815) Apply Ch.Sec
	LLAN-Y-BRI,Hen Gapel (Old Chapel) (1688) now closed
825	LLAN-Y-CRWYS,Pencarreg ZC 1756-1837; C 1765-1837(C); CB 1859-1913(NLW)
	LLIDIADNENNOG WI (1749) Apply Ch.Sec
	MEIDRIM,Cana (1820) now closed
	MEIDRIM,Gibeon (1841) now closed
	MILO WI (1830) Apply Ch.Sec
	MYDDFAI,Capel Seion WI (1816) Apply Ch.Sec
	MYDDFAI,Sardis (1792) now closed
	NANTGAREDIG,Siloam WI (c1824) Apply Ch.Sec
	NEWCASTLE EMLYN,Capel Iwan WI (1723) Apply Ch.Sec Members List 1787-1885 (C)
	PANT-TEG WI (1712) Apply Ch.Sec
	PEN-BOYR Soar WI (1836) Apply Ch.Sec
2517	PEN-BRE (Pembrey) Jerwsalem WI (1812) ZC 1814-37; copies C
	PENCADER (c1695) - see LLanfihangel
	PENTRE-TY-GWYN WI (1749) Apply Ch.Sec
	PEN-Y-BANC,Siloh WI (1817) Apply Ch.Sec
	PEN-Y-GRAIG WI (1748) Apply Ch.Sec
	PEN-Y-GROES,Capel y Sgwar WI (1825) Apply Ch.Sec
	PONTIETS,Nasareth WI (1803) Apply Ch.Sec
	PORT TYWYN,Carmel WI (1828) Apply Ch.Sec
4022	RHYDYCEISIADD,LLangynin WI (1724) ZC 1820-37; copies C
Various	St CLEARS,Bethlehem WI (1744) C 1770-1822,ZC 1821-37,DB 1831-37; copies C
	St CLEARS,Capel Mair WI (1821) Apply Ch.Sec
Various	TRE-LECH ar Bettws,Rock Chapel WI (1705) ZC 1732-1837,B 1788,1789,1834-37; copies C
	TRIMSARAN,Sardis WI (1831) Apply Ch.Sec
	TROEDRHIWALLTWALIS WI (1806) Apply Ch.Sec
	TUMBLE,Bethania C 1800-1837 (C)

DENBIGH

H = Hawarden Record Office
R = Ruthin Record Office

RG4/

ABERGELE,Bodoryn(1825) now closed,replaced by
ABERGELE,Ebenezer WI (1842) inc.St George Chapel
4065   ZC 1823-37;   ZC 1822-27 (R)   Copies SG
ABERGELE,Moelfre WI (1804)   Apply Ch.Sec
BLAENAU WI (1840)   Apply Ch.Sec
BRYMBO,Gyfynys (1805) now closed
3845   ZC 1827-37; copies R
CAERGRWLE (1842) now closed, no trace
CERRIG-y-DRUIDION,Hermon - see also Llangwm
         ZC 1824-37 (R/SG)
DENBIGH,Green Lane WI (1827)   Apply Ch.Sec
DENBIGH,Swan Lane WI (1662)
3488/9   ZC 1763-1837; C 1763-1883(R)
ERBISTOCK,Ebenezer
1722   ZC 1832-37; copies R
GRAIANRHYD,Tabernacle WI (1848)   Apply Ch.Sec
GRAIGFECHAN,Ebenezer WI (1839)   Apply Ch.Sec
LLANARMON (1811) now closed, no trace
LLANDEGLA, Pisgah WI (1817)   Apply Ch.Sec
LLANGOLLEN,Glan-yr-Afon (1812) now closed
3865   ZC 1808-37; ZC 1811-37 (R/SG)
LLANGWYFAN,Ebenezer New Chapel (1830)
3529   ZC 1834-37; copies R/SG
LLANGWM,Capel-y-Groes
1704/3864   ZC 1799-1837; copies R/SG
LLANRWST,Tabernacle (1800)
3444/3775   ZC 1803-37,B 1820-37; ZC 1806-37 (R)
LLANSILIN,Bethesda now closed
4132   ZC 1818-37; copies SG; ZC 1813-37 (R)
NANTGLYN,Salem WI (1833)   Apply Ch.Sec
PENPYLLAU WI,Pisgah (1819)   Apply Ch.Sec
PENTRELLYNCYMER (1812) now closed, no trace
PWLL-GLAS,Salem WI (1837)   Apply Ch.Sec
RHIW,Ebenezer WI (1831)   Apply Ch.Sec
RHOSLLANNERCHRUGOG, Bethlehem WI (1810)
3445   ZC 1808-21; ZC 1810-31 (R)
RHOS-Y-MEDRE,Bethel (1836) now closed
         ZC 1836-37 (R)
RUABON,Independent Chapel
         ZC 1814-37 (R)
RUTHIN,Pen-dref WI (1805)
3867 &   ZC 1810,1818-37,CB 1844-51; ZC 1824-37 (SG)
RG8/104   ZC 1824-68 (R)
TREUDDYN,Penuel (1826) now closed, no trace
TREFOR (1840) now closed, no trace
WREXHAM,Pentre-felin now closed
2784   ZC 1827-37; ZC 1832-37 (H/R)
WREXHAM, Pen-y-Bryn UR (1783)
4126   ZC 1788-1837; copies H/R

DENBIGH (Contd)

2400/3443
WREXHAM,Wern (1805)also known as Salem,Coed Poeth
        ZC 1808-37; copies H/R
YSBYTYIFAN,Bethel,Pentrefoelas ; closed
        ZC 1806-37 (H/R/SG)

FLINT

RG4/
        H = Hawarden Record Office

ABERGELE,Moelfre - see Denbighshire
BAGILLT,Salem WI (1826)
        C 1858-76 (H)
CILCAIN, Salem now closed
        ZC 1808-37 (H)
HOEL MOSTYN ,Whitford (1800-1990)

4092
        ZC 1832-37; copies H ; C 1832-73 (NLW)
HOLYWELL,Chapel St UR (1788)

4082
        ZC 1800-37; copies H; C 1788-1837 (NLW)
HOLYWELL,Seion WI (1842)   Apply Ch.Sec
HOPE,Penuel now closed
        ZC 1827-37
MOLD,Bethel WI (1809)

3876
        ZC 1813-37; copies H; C 1813-63 (NLW)
MOLD,Buckley Mountain Chapel re-formed as UR/PCW

3877
        ZC 1820-36; copies H
NANNERCH,Windymarsh Chapel (1816) now closed
        ZC 1808-37 (H)
NANTGLYN,Salem WI   Apply Ch.Sec
NEWMARKET WI (1700) -see Trelawnyd
PANT-y-BUARTH,Soar   (1837) now closed, no trace
PEN-y-PILLAU - see Denbigh
RHES-y-CAE,Ebenezer WI (1806)

3878
        ZC 1808-38; copies H
RHUDDLAN,Gosen (1831) now closed
        ZC 1810-37 (H)
RHYL,Carmel WI (1839-1991)
RUTHIN,Pend-ref WI (1805)
        C 1824-37 (H)
St ASAPH,Bethlehem (1816) now closed

3480
        ZC 1810-37; copies H
St ASAPH,Waun Chapel WI (1815)
        ZC 1810-37 (H)
SYCHDYN,Bryn Seion WI (1816)   Apply Ch.Sec
TRELAWNYD,John Wynne's Chapel WI
        ZC 1796-1837 (H)
TRELAWNYD,Ebenezer WI
        C 1796-1842 (H)
WAUNGOLEUGOED WI (1815) - see St Asaph,Waun Chapel

```
                     C = Cardiff Record Office
                     S = Swansea Record Office
RG4/
          ABERAFON, Tabernacle    now closed
2293              ZC 1812-37; copies C/S
          ABERCARN,Garn UR (1840)                   Apply Ch.Sec
          ABERDARE,Cwm-Bach WI (1846)
          ABERDARE,Ebenezer WI (1804)
3554              DB 1811-35; copies C/S
          ABERDARE,Nebo WI
3553              DB 1824-35; copies C/S
          ABERDARE,Salem WI -
3770              ZC 1790-1837; copies C/S
          ABERDARE,Siloa WI (1845)                  Apply Ch.Sec
          ABERDARE,Saron WI(1848)                   Apply Ch.Sec
          BLAINA,Berea UR (1842)                    Apply Ch.Sec
          BLAENDULAIS,Soar WI (1826)                Apply Ch.Sec
          BRIDGEND, Bethel Newydd WI (1820)
2544              ZC 1818-37; ZC 1818-47 (C/S)
          BRIDGEND, Castell Newydd
2294              ZC 1785-89 ; copies C/S  - replaced by
          BRIDGEND,Tabernacle WI (1810)
4093              ZC 1801-37; ZC 1801-40 (C/S)
          BRITON FERRY, Bethesda WI(1849)           Apply Ch.Sec
          BRYNAMAN, Gibea WI (1843)                 Apply Ch.Sec
          BRYNCETHIN (1825)   now closed
          BRYN MENYN (1809)   now closed
          CADLE,Bethlehem WI (1840)                 Apply Ch.Sec
          CAERPHILLY,Bethel WI (1848)               Apply Ch.Sec
          CARDIFF,Ebenezer WI )1828)
3781              ZC 1817-37; C 1826-55 (C/S)
          CEFN COED-y-CYMER,Ebenezer (1838)  now closed
          CEFN CRIBWR,Siloam WI (1827)              Apply Ch.Sec
          CLYDACH,Hebron WI (1821)                  Apply Ch.Sec
          COETY,Gilead WI (1821)                    Apply Ch.Sec
          CWMAFAN,Rock Chapel WI (1840)             Apply Ch.Sec
          CWMAFAN,Seion WI (1824)                   Apply Ch.Sec
          CWMLLYNFELL,Capel Newydd WI (c1700)       Apply Ch.Sec
          CYMER AFAN,Hebron WI (1794)
                  Members List 1797-1859 (S)
          CYMER,Rhondda  now closed
                  C 1796-1844 (C)
          DOWLAIS,Bethania WI (1824)
3881              ZC 1825-37; copies C/S
          DOWLAIS,  Bethel  afterwards  Bryn Seion WI  (1829)3880
                  ZC 1829-37; copies C/S
          FELINDRE,Nebo WI (1824)                   Apply Ch.Sec
          GARNANT,Bethel WI (1773)                  Apply Ch.Sec
          GELLIONNEN (1692)  closed, no trace
          GELLIGAER,Craig-bargoed  now closed
3883              ZC 1831-37; copies C/S; C 1831-38 (NLW)
          GLAIS,Seion WI (1841)                     Apply Ch.Sec
          GLANDWR,Siloh WI (1824)                   Apply Ch.Sec
          GLAN-TEG,Ebenezer (1846)  now closed
```

GLYNCORRWG,Cymer (c 1795) now closed
GLYN-NEATH,Addoldy WI (1839)   Apply Ch.Sec
GODRERHOS WI (1753)   Apply Ch.Sec
GROES-WEN,Eglwoysilan WI (1742)
          C 1798-1849; Members Lists 1793-1836 (C)
GWAELODYGARTH,Bethlehem WI (1832)   Apply Ch.Sec
GWAUNCAEGURWEN,Carmel WI (1762)   Apply Ch.Sec
HIRWAUN,Nebo WI (1823)   Apply Ch.Sec
HEOLGERRIG,Salem WI (1840)   Apply Ch.Sec
LLANBLETHIAN,Maendy WI (1749)

3494   ZC 1803-37; copies C/S
LLANFABON,Libanus (1833)   now closed
LLANGIWICK,Pant-Teg WI ; see also Tcilybebyll
3495   ZC 1822-37; copies C/S
LLANGYFELACH, Hebron
3551   ZC 1808-37; copies C/S
LLANGYFELACH,Libanus
3550   ZC 1807-37; copies C/S
LLANGYFELACH,Mynyddbach WI (1762)
3497   ZC 1796-1837; copies C/S; C 1688-1784 (NLW)
LLANGYNWYD,Carmel,Bethesda WI & Siloam (f.1799)
3496   ZC 1809-37; copies C/S
LLANHARAN,Bethlehem WI (1780)
4122/4097   ZC 1777-1814,1829-37 (C/S); C 1849-81 (NLW)
LLAN-HARRI WI (1824)   Apply Ch.Sec
LLANRHIDIAN,Higher Three Crosses Chapel WI (1700)
RG8/105   C 1795-1834; copies C/S
LLANSAMLET,Bethel WI (1818)
3497   ZC 1817-37; copies C/S
LLANTRISANT,Cymmer WI (1809)
          C 1819-44,B 1813-37 (SG)
LLANTWIT MAJOR,Bethesda rep. by Ebenezer in 1815,now UR
1691   ZC 1798-1837,B 1806-20; copies C/S
LLANTWIT MAJOR,Carmel(1838) now closed
MAENDY - see Llanblethian
MAESTEG,Carmel WI (1827)   Apply Ch.Sec
MAESTEG,Siloh (1841)   now closed
MAESTEG,Soar (1842)   now closed

MAES-Y-CWMMER, Tabor UR (1829)   Apply Ch.Sec
MERTHYR TYDFIL,Adullam WI (1830)
3466   ZC 1833-37; copies C/S
MERTHYR TYDFIL,Bethesda (1811) now closed
3500   ZC 1809-37
MERTHYR TYDFIL,Market Square UR (1838) Apply Ch.Sec
MERTHYR TYDFIL, Zoar & Ynys-Gau WI (1801)
3889   ZC 1806-37; copies C/S
MORRISTON,Horeb   (1845)   now   closed
MORRISTON,Libanus (1782) now closed
MYNYDD-BACH - see Llangyfelach
MYNYDD CYNFFIG,Elim (1849) now closed
NANTGARW (1820) now closed

GLAMORGAN (Contd)

```
                NEATH,Ebenezer,Melincwrt WI (1799)      Apply Ch.Sec
                NEATH,Maes-yr-Haf WI (1771)             Apply Ch.Sec
                NEATH,Onllwn WI (1846)                  Apply Ch.Sec
                NELSON,Penuel (1830)   now closed
                OGMORE VALE,Bethania (1847)closed, but try High St UR
                PEN-CLAWDD WI (1818)                    Apply Ch.Sec
                PENTRE-ESTYLL,Siloam WI (1844)          Apply Ch.Sec
                PETERSTONE SUPER-MONTEM - see Llanharan
                PENYDARREN,Horeb (1839) rep. by Williams Mem.UR
                PONTARDAWE,Allt-Wen WI (1750)           Apply Ch.Sec
                PONTSTICILL,Bethlehem (1834) now closed
                PONTYPRIDD,Sardis WI (1834)             Apply Ch.Sec
                PORT TALBOT,Bryn (1847)   now closed
                PORT TALBOT,New Tabernacle WI (1824)    Apply Ch.Sec
                RHIGOS,Calfaria WI (1844)               Apply Ch.Sec
                RHYDRI (1794)   now closed
                RHYD-y-FRO,Saron WI (1844)              Apply Ch.Sec
                St BRIDE'S (1834)   now closed
                SKETTY,Bethel UR nr Swansea (1770)      Apply Ch.Sec
                SKEWEN,Tabernacle WI (1842)             Apply Ch.Sec
                SWANSEA,Capel Seion WI (1843)           Apply Ch.Sec
                SWANSEA,Castle St Chapel (1843)
2295                     ZC 1836-37; copies C/S
                SWANSEA,Castle St Meeting (1814)
RG8/106                  C 1828-35 ; copies C/S
                SWANSEA,Ebenezer (1689)
                         C 1804-74 (NLW)
                SWANSEA,New Ebenezer,Henrietta St WI (1841)
                         Replaced Ebenezer, Regs above refer
                TCILYBEBYLL,LLANGIWICK & LLANGADOCK (see also above)
3900                     ZC 1751-1835,DB 1760-69; copies C/S
                TREOES (1830)
                TRESIMWN (1834)
                TROED-y-RHIW,Seion (1835),now Mount Zion UR
                WATFORD WI,nr Caerphilly (1739)         Apply Ch.Sec
                YSTALYFERA,Pant-Teg WI (1821) - see Llangiwick,Pant-teg
                YSRADFELLTE,Hermon WI (1798)            Apply Ch.Sec
                YSTRADGYNLAIS,Sardis WI (1840)          Apply Ch.Sec

GLAMORGAN - English Chapels
                BETHESDA'R FRO (1806)
                BISHOPSTON,Providence (1805)
                BONVILSTON,Carmel UR (1838)             Apply Ch.Sec
                CARDIFF,New Trinity UR (1640)           Apply Ch.Sec
                CASTELLAU (1843)
                LLANTWIT MAJOR,Ebenezer UR (1815)       Apply Ch.Sec
                MERTHYR TYDFIL,Market Square UR (1840)  Apply Ch.Sec
                MUMBLES,Tabernacle UR (1831)            Apply Ch.Sec
                NEATH,Gnoll Rd UR (1846)                Apply Ch.Sec
                NEWTON NOTTAGE (1828) now closed
                NEWTON,Paraclete CF (1818)
3549                     ZC 1820-37; copies C/S
                NURSTON (1820)
```

GLAMORGAN (Contd)

PARKMILL, Mount Pisgah UR,Gower (1821)   Apply Ch.Sec
PILTON GREEN,Gower (1821)
St MELLONS (1844)
SWANSEA,Canaan (1840)
SWANSEA,Castle St (1814)- see Welsh List
SWANSEA,Burrows Chapel (1789)
TAIHIRION (1822)   now closed, no trace of records

# MERIONETH
            D = Dolgellau Record Office
RG4/
        ABERDOVEY,Capel Mair WI (1840)   Apply Ch.Sec
        BALA,WI (1654)
              C 1770-1839 (D) + some burials
        BARMOUTH,Cutiau WI (1807) see Llanaber,Capel y Cutiau
        BARMOUTH,Siloam WI (1824)
3589   ZC 1827-36; copies D
        BRITHDIR WI (1794)
3899   C 1807-37
        BRYN-CRUG,Nasareth (1845)   closed
        BRYN-CRUG,Saron WI (1837)   Apply Ch.Sec
        CORWEN,Bethesda WI (1825)   Apply Ch.Sec
        CYNWYD,Carmel WI (1839)   Apply Ch.Sec
        DINAS MAWDDWY,Ebenezer WI (1792)
4033   ZC 1797-1837; C 1795-1837 (D)
        DOLGELLAU,Islaw'r-Dref (1823) now closed, no trace
        DOLGELLAU,Tabernacle WI (1808)
3899   ZC 1795-1826,ZC 1826-37; C 1795-1837 (D)
        DYFFRYN ARDUDWY,Rehoboth WI (1826)
3901   ZC 1829-37; copies D
        FFESTINIOG,Bethania WI (1817)   Apply Ch.Sec
        FFESTINIOG,Bethel WI (1840)   Apply Ch.Sec
        FFESTINIOG,Tan-y-Grisiau (1835) now closed, no trace
        FFESTINIOG,Utica WI (1842)   Apply Ch.Sec
        GANLLWYD,Libanus WI (1805)   Apply Ch.Sec
        GELLIOEDD WI (1841)   Apply Ch.Sec
        GLANRAFON,Soar (1848) now closed, no trace
        LLANABER,Capel y Cutiau WI (1807)
3897/99   ZC 1809,1818-37; C 1818-36 (D)
        LLANDDERFEL,Bethel (1825) now closed
3505   ZC 1816-37; copies D
        LLANDRILLO,Hananeel WI (1820)
3505   ZC 1818-37
        LLANEGRYN,Ebenezer WI (1806)   Apply Ch.Sec
        LLANELLTUD,Capel Coffa WI (1802)
3899   C 1807-37
        LLANFACHRETH WI (1843)   Apply Ch.Sec
        LLANFIHANGEL,Tywyn (1817) now closed
        LLANGWM (1830) now closed
        LLANUWCHLLYN,Old Chapel WI (1746)
3902   ZC 1831-37
        LLANUWCHLLYN,Ebenezer
3592   ZC 1814-37

```
          LLANYMAWDDWY,Bethesda WI (1802)          Apply Ch.Sec
          LLWYNGWRIL,Peniel (1808)  now closed
          MACHYNLLETH,Bethsaida (1800) now closed
          MAENTWROG,Gilgal WI (1809)
3593             ZC 1812-37
          PENNAL,Carmel WI (1780)                  Apply Ch.Sec
          RHYD-Y-MAIN,Soar WI (1789)               Apply Ch.Sec
          RHYDYWERNEN,Llanfor WI (1770)
3505             ZC 1821-37
          TRAWSFYNYDD,Ebenezer WI (1840)           Apply Ch.Sec
          TRAWSFYNYDD,Jerwsalem WI (1826)          Apply Ch.Sec
          TRAWSFYNYDD,Pen-y-Stryd (1789)
3474             ZC 1790-1837; copies D
          TY'N-Y-BONT (1730) now closed
          TYWYN (Towyn),Bethesda WI (1800)
2913             ZC 1807-37; copies D; C 1809-1904,M 1840-1902
                                                       (NLW)

          UTICA - see Ffestiniog
```

MONMOUTH

```
          C = Cwmbran Record Office
RG4/
          ABERGAVENNY,Castle St UR (1690)
1241             ZC 1711-1837,B 1806-36
          ABERSYCHAN,Siloh (1838-1963)  no trace of records
          BLAENAVON,Bethlehem CF (1815)            Apply Ch.Sec
          BRYNMAWR,Rehoboth (1646) joined with Nan-y-Glo 1962
          CAERLEON,Village Chapel (1821-92)
3596             ZC 1827-36
          CHEPSTOW,Beulah (1824-1968)
1950             ZC 1828-37; CMB 1865-1958+ Members 1830-1948(C)
          CWMBRAN,Elim UR (1843)                   Apply Ch.Sec
          CWMBRAN,Penywaun UR (1760)               Apply Ch.Sec
          CWMBRAN,Upper Bethel UR (1837)           Apply Ch.Sec
          EBBW VALE,Libanus IC (1839)              Apply Ch.Sec
          EBBW VALE,Saron (1837-1969)
          EBBW VALE,Victoria (1830-1963)
          GARNDIFFAITH,Sardis (1837) now closed
          GARNDIFFAITH,Siloh (1838-1902)
          LLANOVER,Hanover Chapel UR (1644)        Apply Ch.Sec
          LLANVACHES,Tabernacle UR (1639)
1775             ZC 1797-1837,B 1802-37
          LLANVAPLY (1810-1939)
          LLANVIHANGEL,Llantarnam & Penwayne (1817)
1951             ZC 1817-36
          MAESLLECH (1821-87) joined with Caerleon c 1864
          MONMOUTH,St Mary Chapel,Glendower St
1242             ZC 1822-37;  C 1896-1927,M 1895-1927,B 1896-
                                      1928,Ninutes 1858-1930 (C)
          MYNYDDISLWYN,New Bethel UR (1758)        Apply Ch.Sec
          NEWPORT,Hope Chapel (1814-1912)
383              ZC 1815-37
```

MONMOUTH (Contd)

```
                NEWPORT,Mill St Chapel(1640)
                        ZC 1770-1849,DB 1770-1849; C 1770-1849 (SG)
                        C 1770-1928, MB 1871+ (C)
                NEWPORT,Mount Zion (1834)
   383                  ZC 1834-37
                NEWPORT,Tabernacle (1815-1966)
   3597                 ZC 1822-37,B 1831-37; C 1812-1964,M 1838-61,
                        B 1822,Minutes 1830-1965 (C)
                PANTEAGUE New Inn(1756)
   1245                 ZC 1766-1837; C 1766-1837,B 1821-22, Minutes
                        1775-1933 (C)
                PENYMAIN (1640-1970)
   1246                 ZC 1787-1833,B 1787-1835
                PONTNEWYDD ,Ebenezer UR (1740)            Apply Ch.Sec
                PONTYPOOL,Mount Pleasant UR (1835)        Apply Ch.Sec
                RHYMNEY,Sion WI(1821)
   1248                 ZC 1821-37
                RHYMNEY,Moriah WI                         Apply Ch.Sec
                RISCA,Dan-y-Graig UR/PCW (1841)           Apply Ch.Sec
                St ARVAN'S (1830-1952)
                St BRIDE'S,Providence Chapel (1826-1939)
   3764                 ZC 1828-1837
                TREDEGAR,Saron (1813-1991)
   1341                 ZC 1821-37
                TREVETHIN,Babell
   2334                 ZC 1836-37
                TREVETHIN,Bethlehem
   1343                 ZC 1803-37
                TREVETHIN,Ebenezer
2465/2569/2333          ZC 1801-37,B 1829-37
                TRINANT,Horeb EFCC (1841)                 Apply Ch.Sec
                WOLVES NEWTON Chapel (1819-1952)
   1249                 ZC 1819-37
```

MONTGOMERY

```
                L = Llandrindod Wells Record Office
              (No Congregational Records at present held)
   RG4/

                ABERHOSAN WI (1789)                       Apply Ch.Sec
                BERRIW,Ebenezer
   2789                 ZC 1825-37; C 1839-84 (NLW)
                BUILTH WELLS,Hebron CF (1812)             Apply Ch.Sec
                CARNO,Creigfryn WI (1820)                 Apply Ch.Sec
                CEMAIS ROAD,Nebo WI (1816)                Apply Ch.Sec
                CWMLLINE,Sammah WI (1797)
   3904                 ZC 1828-37
                CHERBURY CF - see under Shropshire
                FORDEN,Ebenezer (1826)
   3419                 ZC 1827-36; copies SG
                GLANHAFREN WI (1828)                      Apply Ch.Sec
```

MONTGOMERY (Contd)

	LLANBRYNMAIR,Old Chapel WI (1635)
4068	ZC 1762-1837; C 1762-1876,M 1838-48,B 1843-48
	LLANDISILIO,Dougey Chapel
2571	ZC 1814-37
	LLANDRINDOD WELLS,Christchurch UR (1715)Apply Ch.Sec
	LLANERFYL,Bethel WI (1822) Apply Ch.Sec
	LLANERFYN (1834) now closed, no trace
	LLANFAIR CAEREINION,Ebenezer WI (1814)
3906	ZC 1811-37 ;C 1818-47 (NLW)
	LLANFYLLIN,Pen-dref WI (1635)
3472	ZC 1764-1821
	LLANFYLLIN,Soar (1830) now closed
2335	ZC 1819-37
	LLANIDLOES,Zion UR (1821)
3907	ZC 1810-37; C 1818-37 (NLW)
	LLANRHAIADR,The Tabernacle UR (1688)
4073	ZC 1810-37
	LLANRHAIADR-Y-MOCHNANT WI (1808) Apply Ch.Sec
	LLANSANTFRAID,Bethesda WI (1829) Apply Ch.Sec
	LLANSILIN,Bethesda WI (1814) Apply Ch.Sec
	LLANWDDYN,Sardis WI (1809) Apply Ch.Sec
	LLANWDDYN,Saron WI (1825) Apply Ch.Sec
	LLANWNNOG,Seion WI (1826) Apply Ch.Sec
	LLANWRTHWL,Penuel UR (1832) Apply Ch.Sec
	LLANWRYN,Saron WI (1836) Apply Ch.Sec
	MACHYNLLETH, Graig Chapel WI (1788)
3598/2550/4036	ZC 1791-1813, 1854-57; CB 1842-65 (NLW)
	MAENGWYNEDD,Bryn-y-Groes WI (1824) Apply Ch.Sec
	MEIFOD,Bethel WI (1814) Apply Ch.Sec
	NANTMEL, Carmel UR (1821) Apply Ch.Sec
	NEWTOWN, Bwlch-y-Fridd CF (1781) Apply Ch.Sec
	NEWTOWN,Park St UR (1734) Apply Ch.Sec
	NEWTOWN, Milford Road WI (1847) Apply Ch.Sec
	PENIEL WI (1830) Apply Ch.Sec
	PENLLYS WI (1822) Apply Ch.Sec
	PENNANT,Bethania WI (1782)
4100	ZC 1829-37
	PONTROBERT,Seion WI (1824) Apply Ch.Sec
	RHOSGOCH,Hermon CF (1839) Apply Ch.Sec
	WELSHPOOL,New St Chapel UR/PCW (1794)
3908	ZC 1788-1837
	WELSHPOOL,Penarth WI (1789) Apply Ch.Sec
	Y FOEL,Beersheba WI (1800) Apply Ch.Sec

PEMBROKE   H = Haverfordwest Record Office

RG4/

	ANTIOCH WI (1846) Apply Ch.Sec
	BRAWDY,Trefgarn (1686)
4039	ZC 1809-37; copies H ; C 1796-1830 (H)
	BRYNBERIAN WI (1690) Apply Ch.Sec
	CARFAN WI (1797) Apply Ch.Sec
	CLUNDERWEN,Bethesda WI (1797) Apply Ch.Sec

	CRUNDALE UR (1838)	Apply Ch.Sec
	DALE (c1838) closed, no trace	
	DINAS CROSS,Gedeon WI (1813)	Apply Ch.Sec
	FELINDRE,Cana WI (1810)	Apply Ch.Sec
	FISHGUARD, Tabernacle (1790)	
3913	ZC 1807-37; copies H ;	
	DB 1788-1837	
	FREYSTROP,Bethel CF (1830)	
	ZC 1831-37 (H)	
	GLYNDWR WI (1712) - see LLANFYRNACH	
	GOODWICK,Rhos-y-Caerau WI (1724)	
3913	ZC 1775-1837,DB 1788-1837; copies H	
	HAVERFORDWEST,Albany,The Green Meeting UR (1638)	
4040/3914	ZC 1705-1836; copies H; C 1837-47,B 1655	
	-1743 (H) ; Members List 1655-1900 (H)	
	HAVERFORDWEST,Crundale - see CRUNDALE	
	HAVERFORDWEST, Keyston UR (1787)	
	ZC 1730-1864,B 1808-28 (H)	
	HAVERFORDWEST, The Tabernacle CF (1774)	
3475	ZC 1780-1837; copies H ; C 1836-1869 (H)	
	HAVERFORDWEST,Zion's Hill UR (1823)	
	ZC 1821-37 (H)	
	LITTLE HAVEN (1812) now closed, no trace	
	LLANDDEWI FELFFRE,Bethel (1824) closed, no trace	
	LLANDEILO WI (1714)	Apply Ch.Sec
	LLANDYSILIO,Pisgah WI (1826)	
2489	ZC 1828-37; copies H	
	LLANFYRNACH,Glandwr WI (1712)	
3915/4077	C 1785-1824,ZC 1822-37,B 1785-1808;copies H	
	C 1746-94 (NLW)	
	LLANGLYDWEN,Hebron	
	ZC 1818-37 (H)	
	LLAN-TEG UR (1814)	Apply Ch.Sec
	LLAYS CASTLE & SPITTAL now closed	
2490	C 1790-1830,ZC 1819-37	
	LLWYN-YR-HWRDD WI (1806)	Apply Ch.Sec
	MAENCLOCHOG,Old Chapel WI (1790)	
	ZC 1788-1970 (NLW) ; ZC 1788-1985 (H)	
	MAENCLOCHOG,Siloh WI (1842)	Apply Ch.Sec
	MAENCLOGHOG,Tabernacle WI (1846)	Apply Ch.Sec
	MANORBIER (1822) no trace	
	MATHREY,Rehoboth WI (1841)	Apply Ch.Sec
	MILFORD HAVEN, The Tabernacle UR (1808)	
2781	ZC 1796-1837; copies H	
	MILFORD HAVEN,Tiers Cross UR (1815)	Apply Ch.Sec
	MOYLE GROVE,Bethel (1691) closed	
	NARBERTH,Tabernacle UR (1817)	Apply Ch.Sec
	NARBERT,Templeton UR (1818)	Apply Ch.Sec
	NEVERN, Glanrhyd	
	ZC 1831-37 (H)	
	NEWPORT,Ebenezer WI (1740)	
4072	ZC 1775-1837; copies H	
	NEWPORT,Gedeon WI (1813) - see Dinas Cross	

```
                PEMBROKE,Nebo (1832) now closd, no trace
                PEMBROKE,Tabernacle UR (1811)              Apply Ch.Sec
                PEMBROKE DOCK,Albion Sq (1824)  now Trinity UM
3056                  ZC 1825-37; copies H
                PEN-Y-BONT,Ford Chapel (1807)
                      ZC 1819-37 (H)
                PEN-Y-GROES WI,Whitchurch (c1770)
                      ZC 1785-1837,B 1785-1824 (H)
                RHOS-Y-CAERAU - See Goodwick
                ROSEMARKET,Tabernacle UR (1801)            Apply Ch.Sec
                St DAVID'S,Berea WI (1833)                 Apply Ch.Se
                St DAVID'S,Rhodiad (1784)
4071                  ZC 1799,1810-37; ZC 1799-1829 (H)
                Replaced by Ebenezer WI (1815)
                      ZC 1814-37 (H)
                St DOGMAEL'S WI (1828)                     Apply Ch.Sec
                St FLORENCE,Bethel WI (1800)
3919                  ZC 1801-37; ZC 1803-37 (H)
                St ISHMAEL'S,Sardis (1829) now closed  - see also Tenby
                      ZC 1803-37 (H)
                SAUNDERSFOOT (1838)  closed, no trace of records
                SOLVA,Old Meeting (1798)  now closed
2341/2 & 3920         ZC 1780-1837, C 1814-31;C 1814-37 (H)
                TEMPLETON (1818)  closed, no trace
                TENBY,Tabernacle (1822) - see also St Ishmael
                      ZC 1803-37 (H)
                TREFGARN - see Brawdy
                TREWYDDEL WI (c1743)                       Apply Ch.Sec
                TY-RHOS WI (1817)                          Apply Ch.Sec
                WOLFSDALE,Bethel (1826)
                      ZC 1827-36,B 1828-40;  copies H;  CMB 1844-56
                                                              (NLW)
```

RADNOR

RG4/
```
                NANTMEL,Carmel & Pendrel Chapels  now closed
4005a                 ZC 1830-37
                OLD RADNOR,Gore Chapel  now closed
2344                  ZC 1805-36,B 1827-36
```

OTHER SOURCES

The scope of this booklet in covering Congregational records in England & Wales has been largely dictated by two factors ; the basis being the holdings in the Public Record Office, and the fact that the Congregational Union of England & Wales has dominated the scene for one hundred and forty years – an era almost as long as St Catherine's House.

It would be wrong however not to comment on two other areas of research which lie outside the present project.

In 1850 there were almost one hundred Congregational churches in Scotland. Today only six remain as members of the United Reformed Church, two of these being survivors from 1850. The Congregational Federation have only one Scottish chapel, Pilgrim Church at Airdrie.

Most of the Scottish churches are 19th century in origin, and therefore what records survive do not go back very far. It is known that Congregational registers and Minute Books have been deposited with the main Scottish Record Office in Edinburgh, and with the Strathclyde Record Office. Other record offices in Scotland should also be checked.

It should be remembered that the records in the General Register Office in Edinburgh – the Scottish equivalent of St Catherine's House do not commence until 1855, and therefore local registers if kept before then are important.

There was also a smaller Congregational presence in Ireland; the Irish Archives Service should know what records survive.

The second source is the Missionary arm of the Congregationalists.

The London Missionary Society was founded towards the end of the eighteenth century, and together with the Colonial Missionary Society established mission stations around the world. The main areas were China, India, the South Seas, South & Central Africa, and the Caribbean whilst the CMS concentrated its efforts on the Americas and Australia.

Most of the missionary historical records are now held at the School for Oriental & African Studies, University of London, Malet St WC1 7HP.

The LMS was subsequently renamed the Congregational Council for World Mission, but since 1972 the word 'Congregational' has been dropped and the CWM is currently supported by both the URC and the Congregational Federation.